ABDUCTED BY LICHEN

AN INTERSPECIES JOURNEY OF LOVE, HEALING, AND WISDOM

GLENN SIEGEL

FOR
MARION, NORMAN, AND BEATZIE
LOVE IN THE INVISIBLE REALM

CONTENTS

WISDOM

INTRODUCTION

Lichen. An unlikely subject I suppose. And yet, this journey into the remarkable world of lichen now reveals its place as one of our most ancient and wise ancestors. This understated being holds the wisdom of the ages and may light the way for the urgently needed transformation of our human trajectory. If we could humbly choose to attend and listen, one of nature's most overlooked or ignored beings can serve as a guide toward our own awakening and enlightenment.

Lichen lives in harmony with its environment and often endures without significant nourishment. This remarkable being can survive inhospitable conditions of extreme variations in climate, aridity, geography, and epochs of profound deprivation. Through its symbiotic make-up, Lichen demonstrates the power and intelligence of collaborative relationship beyond competition or domination.

I don't know why Lichen chose me as a translator to bring her wisdom to others of my species. That will likely remain a mystery. What I do know is that my journey with Lichen began with an irresistible immersion in Love. Within that compelling loving container, I was guided unwittingly into my deepest psychic wound, previously impenetrable through even the most skillful psychotherapy and psychoanalysis. This descent into woundedness and ultimate healing required that I pass through a portal of disavowed grief so threatening that my death seemed ominously near.

No wonder I was well defended for decades. Ultimately this unplanned interspecies journey transformed my previously unhealed wound into a sacred gift now ready to share with others. Lichen helped me circumvent my egoic protections in an other-than-human process, and my gratitude and call to reciprocate is strong. This book is born of that desire and through my particular experience as an example, it also serves to illustrate the possibility of interspecies relationship for deepest healing. I choose to capitalize Lichen throughout the book as a symbol of reverence and gratitude for my apprenticeship to this extraordinary being.

The etymology of "lichen" is from the Greek "to lick" and on to Latin, where it became "lichen." Lichen seems to "lick stones and bark of trees"—a sensually evocative image. Imagine licking the surface of all of the earth, all types of land from arctic to desert to tropic wetness. What a rich range of tastes! How magnificent to be in such intimate connection with much of the surface of the planet. Living on water vapor and photons of light, Lichen's subtle and delicate way of interacting with the cosmos is sublime. The fungal elements offer algae a place to photo-commune with built in structural protection. What a caring shelter this is; one could say "loving" since it is a relationship of mutual flourishing.

Lichen's unique achievement of spanning the deepest chasm of "separateness" between two (or more) biologically unrelated organisms is nothing short of miraculous. This accomplishment, symbiosis, is foundational for the evolution of all ensuing species, including our own. Relationship as the basis of evolutionary success is quite contrary to the idea of competition for survival that characterizes our typical understanding of evolution.

Once in that symbiotic union, the fungi are no longer structurally identical to fungi yet remain functional as providers of support, protection, and contributor of minerals and water to the symbiotic union. And the photobiont, now embedded in the overall Lichen structure, loses its separate algal or cyanobacterial distinctions but still continues to provide the nourishing energy of photosynthesis to the whole being. Neither betrays its own essence while contributing to the loving union of the symbiosis.

Lynn Margulis in her 1998 visionary book *Symbiotic Planet: A New Look at Evolution* writes:

> *Symbiogenesis brings together unlike individuals to make larger, more complex entities. Symbiogenetic life-forms are even more unlike than their unlikely "parents." "Individuals" permanently merge and regulate their reproduction. They generate new populations that become multiunit symbiotic new individuals. These become "new individuals" at larger, more inclusive levels of integration. Symbiosis is not a marginal or*

Through this life-long symbiotic commitment, Lichen survives in conditions where neither fungus nor alga may have survived before. I can see this as a place in the natural system where Love is palpably visible, and an example of wisdom present to us all in tangible form.

For those of us open to fully accepting this extraordinary marriage of inherently different "individuals," it may even confirm the theological assertion that the essence of 'God' or Mystery is Love. Relationship as Love. At the least, it inarguably proves the value of diversity that we revere, not simply tolerate.

Perhaps one of the reasons Lichen is so peripheral, so unnoticed is because its existence is so antithetical to the essential movement and quest for change that our culture thrives on. Lichen has no outward variation through the seasons, grows imperceptibly, and outlasts almost everything else in the living system. This is not the ephemeral, surface seduction of the culture, so Lichen does not attract most eyes.

The cycles we witness and evolved from do seem to hold many apparent opposites, ultimately life and death, so as the culture seeks immortality and ageless youth, we also move closer to extinction. What irony that is!

Language, communication, speed, reading that stimulates imagination— it would all be so beautiful, if it weren't for the backdrop of self-destruction through lack of reciprocity. But then is the juxtaposition of these opposites necessary to create the tension of life? Is that where energy arises?

Although targeted as the most dangerous diseases of our time, cancer, heart disease, and numerous other medically labeled conditions, are only surface symptoms of a vastly more devastating threat to our existence. This killer is none other than *disconnection* in all its forms. Many of us live within the illusion that we are all separate beings, free to live an independent quest without awareness of what ultimately sustains us. There is a belief in "getting ahead" or succeeding through accumulation and elaborate constructions for security, in addition to speed of movement, and "saving time." There is no wisdom in this. In contrast, Lichen is a supreme teacher of stillness and silence within the framework of deep connection and through this way of being has endured millennia.

In Western dominant culture, we have lost the sense of reciprocity that allows a living system to flourish. Understanding reciprocity allows for the crucial insight that all beings are profoundly interconnected and that no one species has superiority. There is no hierarchy of value on this planet, in this cosmos, but instead a vast and mysterious network in which innumerable diverse beings contribute to the overall movement, evolution, and awakening of the whole in unique and essential ways.

This disconnection from our natural home is the inevitable consequence of an even more insidious form of alienation. We are disconnected from our own inner resources. Our emotions are suppressed; our dreams and imagination are trampled and dismissed. Then, in our misery, promises of relief are delivered in the form of myriad external cures. Few of us continue to realize our own inner capacities as our culture diverts us from believing in them.

There is a pharmacologic intervention to assuage just about anything experienced as discomfort. This goes well beyond basic help in disease management or treatment. The vast profits from this venture are partly funneled back into synthesizing even more of these so-called health aids despite the toxicities and long-term damages that many of these substances deliver.

If that were not enough, we continue to turn further away from the diverse offerings of our living system and settle for the soul-numbing homogeneity of digital distractions, most television offerings, and the multitude of consumer products flooding us daily. As we rely more blindly on these external, man-made concoctions and technological distractions, we tragically disconnect from the wealth of our unique human gifts. It is a grievous process as one luminous infant after another is molded into the next generation of consumer, with only a dim awareness remaining of their unique, creative gifts.

Lichen has such a different way of inhabiting this earth. More ubiquitous in habitats than even humans, Lichen endures through eons by living in reciprocity, not depleting resources, growing quite slowly, suspending its energy production and consumption when conditions are harsh and devoid of nourishment, and surviving through collaboration. This is a Wisdom Elder for us if we choose to pay attention. But so far, Lichen's way is so peripheral, so "boring," so constant, so independent of trend or technological invention, that its wisdom is of little or no interest to most humans.

We see this blindness to reciprocity in most of our culture's institutions, and we continue to squander the potential of humanity from one generation to the next. Our children are raised to be consumers, exploiters of natural resources, and cavalier dumpers of toxic waste back into the environment that both generates and sustains us.

And what of beauty? It would seem that the wild and natural world still holds the power there and that man-made items can never reach that depth of response within us, born of our origins. However, many people have had such persistent deprivation of exposure to natural wildness, that art's interpretation of nature through the artist is as good as it gets.

Even those of us who venture out to more natural settings often negate this experience with something plugged in our ears to carry technology with us. The implication is that natural sights and sounds are not stimulating enough for us and somehow the repeated listening to familiar sounds or music is deemed more "entertaining." It is as though we need an antidote to what would otherwise be a "boring" encounter with nature. There is a diabolical quality to this method of consumerism as the very items that are experienced as stimulating or entertaining are in truth devastatingly soul numbing in their virulent homogeneity.

In contrast, there is no routine of sound or sight or smell in the wild. Each moment is a new offering of infinite variation and if we attend without human-made distractions, the benefits may be profound. Our creative possibilities are revisited, the risk inherent in unpredictability is embraced, and our path takes unexpected turns beyond what we would have designed left to a routine.

But this would not be good for business as usual so a tight hold over us is maintained as new and seductive consumer products are introduced. What seems new and interesting has little or no depth compared to the natural living systems around us, but these products successfully seem to catch our attention; apparently as a culture we have not matured beyond this susceptibility to the new and shiny and clever.

Lichens know better. Through their extraordinary communion in the face of what at times might be lethal conditions, these beings have endured for hundreds of millions of years. Will we be able to say the same? Because Lichens have a photosynthetic component through their algal or cyanobacterial elements, they produced oxygen so early in evolutionary history that we would not have emerged without the atmospheric foundation they helped generate.

This book arises out of gratitude to one of our most ancient ancestors. Having been infused with Lichen's presence for several years now, I've wrestled with my egoic protections in order to become an apprentice to this omnipresent being. Lichen speaks to those who listen, and this book explores the primary teachings made available to me and the healing love-infused journey I've been fortunate to travel.

LOVE

"Remember. I came to you in Love." **Lichen**

WHY ME?

Early May 2015. I'm in a Ponderosa pine forest above 7,000 feet in Northern New Mexico and I've come here to wander, to saunter. My movement is slow as I intentionally shed the defensive shields that have been girding me from myriad urban assaults. I find my way with curiosity to a notable change in the land where a demarcation captures my scanning vision. It is a surprisingly linear and clean border for such a wild place.

On one side is an expanse of low, deep green vegetation, almost carpet-like in its thorough cover of the land. With closer scrutiny I see it is punctuated with tiny pink rimmed, bell-shaped white flowers drooping from thin arched stems. This spread of green is uniform except for a few granite stones, one of which I choose for a pillow buffered only by my small pack. I am drawn to lie down in this inviting softness and in doing so my gaze re-orients more deeply into this green and white-pink network.

Innumerable bees have also been attracted here and I watch closely as they sample scores of blooms, seemingly in chaos but still focused on their industry. No doubt they are productive even though the brevity of their contact with each blossom would seem to prevent any significant accumulation of nectar.

As I settle into the comforting hum of this activity, my view shifts upward and my attention to every other sound is heightened. The humming bee drone gives me a foundation to take in the natural improvisations of tree top swishes in the wind and the relentless water collisions with stones in the nearby, but out of sight, creek. I am in a reverie of sound, as the shapes of so many beings--branches, pine needles, stones, wings--sketch out the contours of this place by fielding and re-launching the invisible air borne vibrations that softly map out their surface borders. I am enveloped, open, and undefended.

While in this state, so rare and fragile, I now notice the other world across the line, that sharp demarcation that enticed me here initially. The pines are dense there and no green thrives underneath them in the complete shade they create. These Ponderosas are regally tall and unerringly vertical with mosaic bark sporting orange irregular panels divided by grout-like black borders. Quite stylish, in their way.

As I lie here feeling blessed by these two distinct rooms in my new temporary home, a small being several feet up the torso of a distant pine glimmers at me and beckons; I am compelled to respond. I rise and am drawn by an unfamiliar magnetism focused on the center of my chest and intensifying as I tentatively walk closer. My body leads me there. The air thickens with a kind of embracing texture. I feel welcome, sensing some kind of intangible, invisible and healing energy emanating from the source I now eagerly and wholeheartedly seek. Only a few feet away now, both coating and draping from a short, life-less branch that protrudes horizontally is an intricate pale-green growth of Lichen. I am surprised to discover that this is what calls me, and I feel completely entranced.

I now face her just below eye level. I instinctively feel this being as feminine, relationally focused, and sensual. At first, I admire the freedom she has to venture into all spatial dimensions using the branch merely as an anchor; she adheres gently for support without damage. Her shape appears uninhibited, unregimented, with a random approach to both air and light. The subtlety of her color, a modest gray-green, suggests the maturity and wisdom of longevity and endurance. She is an Elder.

I then begin to feel her energy traveling through my entire body, arousing me sensually. This is surprisingly erotic. The pull is powerful, and I am compelled to make physical contact. My choice is to share the growth of my own bearded chin with her filamentous arms. We intermingle in that way, my white chin hairs and her green fingers joining in charged connection. The distance between such divergent living species across eons of time and evolution is crossed with ease. I am electrified and awed, immersed in a state I can only name as reverent Love. In this blissful joining, my lips venture softly into contact and the joy deepens.

I still have a shred of ego witnessing this unlikely, unexpected communion and what would clearly be judged culturally as madness. Fortunately, that perspective has no hold over me and I feel no inclination or pull back into conformity. A deep longing is being met, a knowing that this experience of Love is what creates and drives the cosmos. I am fortunate, gifted with this glimpse of deep interconnection while realizing simultaneously the illusion of separateness so dangerously threatening the survival of humanity. All of this awareness comes to me in seconds.

There is no wasted time in this unitive state and almost immediately I give voice to a vow of betrothal. I am committed to all that this connection brings, despite its foreignness and mystery; there is no ambivalence. My thoughts have no opening to intrude or dissuade me as I serenely bask in this loving energy. I am fully present and exquisitely alive.

***

Eventually, after some unmeasured span of time, I remember the group of other humans waiting for me and I slowly and wistfully detach from this sublime connection with Lichen. A solemn sense of gravity overtakes me as I reverently step away. This slowness of movement persists as I walk profoundly altered down the forested aisle in my state of betrothal. I feel as though I have been guided through a kind of marriage ceremony, not yet aware of what is to come from this union.

My consciousness expands into the awareness that I belong to a vast network; I am not a truly separate being. Embedded in this paradigm shifting awareness is a faint but unmistakable inkling of great and daunting responsibility. Although the reverent love and beauty of this encounter stays with me, there is also a foreboding trace of terror. I recognize that I have a consuming task ahead, but what is it?

***

"I am a relational Being; it is my essential nature; this is what sustains me and allows the cosmic Love to flow through me. Learn from this. Again, remember it is Love that brings you here." **Lichen**

Like a sequence of cartoon cels, I sometimes see movement through living as a series of discreet or apparently disconnected events, only vaguely related. Time may either elongate or abbreviate these events, yet while immersed in any one of them, the preceding ones all but disappear. Of course, I know there is a thread of connection running through it all, but my conscious awareness does not hold this truth without great effort. My inclination to package, wall off, and nearly forget all that comes before is disturbing. It makes me an accomplice to the cultural disease of our time, a susceptible and active participant in all that I know is damaging and potentially destroying humanity and all other life on the planet. And so, I too am not immune to the illusion of separateness and all of the devastation it brings.

Most of us cannot hold the truth of flow as we compartmentalize our lives. If we could, we might realize that profound relatedness and interconnection is the essence of life and all phenomena, whether animate or not. Living in that awareness, how could we exploit, damage, neglect, or in any way be blind to the source of our own genesis and ongoing sustenance?

Humans apparently have the unique capacity to imagine, and with this gift the power to create and shape the future. This extraordinary achievement of evolution, the human imagination, must be harnessed and not abused. Within this gift the survival of the living systems of the planet itself is at stake. Although imagination is often future directed, perhaps one responsibility inherent in this ability includes revering what precedes us. We evolved from the integration of many previous life forms, particularly symbiotic relationships. Lichen is an early pioneer of this extraordinary achievement, the legacy of which is identifiable in our own bodies. We have only to consider the fact that the mitochondria within each of our cells, the essential energy producers, were once bacteria. Only the wildest "imagination" could have transformed this independent organism into the mitochondrial energy creators driving the life of complex beings such as humans. There are numerous other examples of symbiosis throughout the plant and animal kingdoms.

Imagination has thus preceded us, using the cosmos as the myriad variations, sizes, life cycles, habitats, forms, shapes, etc. so blatantly illustrate. It could even be said that humans have incorporated the imagination of creation just as we have done through our symbiotic connection with former bacteria. Is this another perspective on what it might mean to have been created in the "image" of God? Is it this imaginative, creative, and even generative capacity that is in God's image?

I turn to Lichen as these realizations unfold. This ancient being, one of the earliest land dwellers, teaches us about the enduring power of relationship, of connection, through symbiotic transformation. Eons before "higher" forms of Animalia evolved, in part through the incorporation of bacteria en route to mitochondria, fungus harnessed the energy of photosynthesis through the incorporation of algae or cyanobacteria, and their genius capacity for weaving photons of light into life giving energy.

What is crucial here, is the life giving, life sustaining, and life enhancing power of relatedness. Lichen, arguably one of the "lowliest" visible life forms to many people and thus usually ignored in the quest for grander scenic beauty and drama, holds the key, the foundational truth, the fuel our imaginations need to shape a future compatible with the ongoing existence of the living system of this planet. Lichen has endured hundreds of millions of years in almost every planetary environment. It can even survive significant time in the vacuum void conditions of outer space as experiments have shown. In comparison, the present trajectory of humanity may prove to be a mere flimsy fad.

Lichen is unobtrusive, still, and silent, eclipsed by mountain and ocean vistas, singing birds, graceful predators, eroding powers of wind and water, and the intensity and heat of sunlight. Yet, it has called me to deliver a message of deep healing and transformation, even salvation. In my "marriage" commitment to Lichen, this is the vow I take, a promise, which in the words of poet David Whyte, *"it would kill [me] to break."* I become a translator, a speaker of Lichen's great wisdom using the language of human culture as the medium to express it on behalf of a being so still and silent, that it may not be heard or revered for the profound guidance it models.

Like any relationship, this one has challenges for me, specifically because of Lichen's silence and apparent unresponsiveness. How do I live in a 'marriage' without the currency of human interplay? In most connections, human or other animal, there is typically some identifiable responsiveness, but in Lichen's silent presence and immobility, I am forced to sit deeply with myself without reprieve. I realize during these silent spells, how much I rely on projection to avoid such discomfort. By trying to understand Lichen, I project human characteristics onto this blank screen so I can react in a familiar way as I would with a more interactive being. This doesn't work of course, and I must eventually face myself more fully. Projection offers me an escape, an avoidance of sitting with my own reality. If I can be immersed positively or negatively in another's words or actions, I can avoid facing the illusions I hold about myself. Relentless reactions to and judgment of others are powerful habits to break but these judgments and distortions separate us from reality. And since this illusion of separateness distances us from awareness of interconnection, we no longer see ourselves as members of an Earth community. From this perspective, we are then capable of destroying our environment and are actively doing so. How do we reconcile our distancing projective process with the truth of interconnectedness and the essential compassion needed for a habitable future?

How did ancient fungi make the leap from separateness to a deeply collaborative and transformative union with such a foreign being as an alga? It had to relinquish its former structural self to do so. It's border, walls of distinctive difference, had to give way. Was/is an imagined future at play here?

Although on the surface I hear nothing from Lichen in the familiar currency of language emanating from sound creation, I realize a subtler and more powerful process is at work. Lichen has granted me the privilege of being an instrument, a vessel of expression, leaving it up to me to translate and therefore transmit her wisdom via a language understandable by humans who are not otherwise listening. What allowed me to actually listen? Although I can't answer this question, I'm grateful that it happened.

What appears as only Lichen's indifference, and actually is indifference at one level, offers profound guidance uncluttered by the usual human desires, needs, wants, fears, anxieties, doubts, longings, yearnings, sorrows, joys, envies, jealousies, defenses, attacks, and obsessions that shape our choices. In other words, Lichen does not strategize or manipulate, does not plan or control and has no agenda. Her path is enlightened, fully present, authentic, and a model for us all.

In Lichen's presence, as I grapple with the stillness, the silence, and the indifference, I know that I am witnessing a supreme holder of longevity, a pioneer of living on this planet that has forged the way for other so-called "higher" life forms. What starts out as my frustration with Lichen's apparent lack of response soon dissolves into gratitude when my awareness expands beyond the desire for the immediate and essentially small appeasements I am accustomed to relying on.

Such is the thin veneer of conversation with the world our culture teaches us. Amid all the raucous, glamorous, glittering, ephemeral luxuries that relentlessly beckon and distract, Lichen staunchly holds to the deeper, enduring truths of profound interconnection and love. As I reflect on Lichen's core approach, I'm able to muster some resistance to the pressures to conform, consume, accumulate, follow, or succumb to this toxic homogeneity so cruelly inflicted upon us all.

What passes as energy in our typical cultural activity is in fact deadening, numbing, and dangerously disconnecting. We are lured into cultural indoctrination forgetting our uniqueness, or as James Hillman writes, our "soul's code." It is through realizing and living out our unique essence that our true and indestructible wealth lays. Were we to fully inhabit ourselves and give voice to our wild natures, no commodity, bank account, or preservation of youth could compare to the vast wealth within each of us. Our culture misleads us into the belief that we are drab, deteriorating, and dispensable so that we desperately clutch at one adornment, anti-aging, emerging commodity after the next; money is the means for these ends and of course the end justifies the means. Exploitation and greed abound in this scheme.

Lichen's life course is the antithesis of these cultural aims. It does not change with the times, except over eons of evolution, does not buffer itself from the rest of the natural world, makes no noise, is not rushing to get anywhere else, does not demand attention, is not on a quest for eternal youth, and does not typically harm or exploit other beings. As a result of its non-compelling nature, Lichen is often ignored, or is at best seen as peripheral in the human quest for grandeur.

Lichen is anything but drab as it takes seemingly infinite shapes and forms, ranges through the most intense palette of hues equaling or surpassing any colorful dyes, and adorns even the most barren landscapes, stones, and dead branches. All the while it is enriching our atmosphere with life sustaining oxygen in addition to sometimes creating new substrate soil for other beings to grow. When I pay attention to all of what Lichen teaches and gives, many of the creations of human culture that thrive on subjugating our uniqueness and prey upon our vulnerabilities collapse into the very emptiness from which they arise in the first place.

After my first encounter of reverent love with Lichen, I began to exuberantly share stories of this new-found relationship with others. Many people are intrigued by this unlikely pairing and ask questions. Most say they have not really noticed Lichen before or have not distinguished it from moss, lumping these distinctly different beings together.

As this process unfolds in those open to witnessing my journey with Lichen, new-found and often playful responses are shared with me. I receive photographs from people who think of me when they notice Lichen while wandering in nature. These images come from several places around the world and when I receive them, I'm awed by the spread of connection this unlikely encounter in a Ponderosa pine forest spawned. As this sense of a living family is growing, the realization of interconnectedness is widening, and within that awareness, little by little, there is a renewed sense of hope. If this can happen through one of the most unnoticed, disregarded beings, the possibility for this healing process on a larger scale is ever more present.

There is something essential or central in the human imagination that is stimulated or evoked when what has been previously overlooked or seen as insignificant is suddenly revealed in its primacy. Perhaps it is like an archetypal Cinderella story. What had been relegated to a shadowy existence, eclipsed by the more overt displays of other beings, landscapes, or bodies of water, now suddenly comes into its own. The power and beauty now acknowledged is profound. This shift in perception from the hidden to the light of awareness is exhilarating and releases previously bound energy that was used to contain, separate, and dismiss a part of creation.

I continue to apprentice myself to Lichen's guidance. As my knowledge increases, I can spread Lichen's wisdom to others with both broader and deeper strokes. But most importantly it is the encompassing Love that I experienced in Lichen's presence that guides me. Love is the essential component of this apprenticeship and what I seek to live into with deeper presence. Perhaps like Lichen, I can become of vessel of Love flowing through me too.

***

I didn't know there was such a thing as a Lichenologist in the world of biological science. Of course there would be, but my ignorance just shows how peripheral Lichen was to me, not even significant enough for me to assume it warranted its own field of study. In that light, it's all the more puzzling that I was summoned and shown my place in the web of cosmic Love as an invitation to telling the story of this ancient being.

I now know scientists are also exploring Lichen and its importance in evolution, but since I'm not a scientist, I'm coming from a different perspective, one apparently Lichen has chosen for me. I've never thought of myself as a translator; my Spanish is adequate, but even with that I could never take on the role of translator. Yet, that is precisely what I'm being asked to do, and to translate from a language of silence and stillness, without even body language to infer from.

Maybe that's not entirely true. Lichen tells me about its extraordinary body whenever I'm in her presence. Whether flat and crusty (crustose), leafy and undulating (foliose), or dramatically draping in filaments (fruticose), Lichen always beckons me to pay attention, be still, listen, sometimes ask questions, and at other times, share my own challenging experiences. After all, Lichen has seen, weathered, and lived through more than I can imagine including ages when other beings were quite different than those living now. Lichen is giving me a window into the distant past, the very beginnings of life on land. I believe I may have been chosen for this gift both for my own healing from a disconnected, disjointed, emotional past, and even more importantly, for me to deliver crucial messages to other humans. The survival of our species depends on learning from this model of living.

Experiencing the power of such a vast network of Love during our first encounter gave me a dose of curative healing and belonging. I can't imagine a greater gift, so Lichen's offering must be reciprocated by spreading the word as I learn it, and more importantly spreading Love as I am able. I'm still an early apprentice no doubt, but Lichen apparently believes in me and has chosen me for this task.

Just as I end a multi-decade profession and have no further pressing career, parental supervision, or financial debts to shape my schedule, I find myself suddenly indentured, willingly but with trepidation, to what feels like an unending responsibility on a great planetary scale. All from this unobtrusive but powerful holder of living history.

"Why me?' is certainly a question I ponder. Is there something Lichen recognized in my psyche that makes me her choice? When I search to understand this, Lichen's silence emerges as a crucial element in this dynamic.

In my own history, silence was a cruel injury, a betrayal, and within the void it created, my wound deepened. My early childhood was filled with good fortune and opportunity, and I remember feeling cherished by both of my parents. Mysteriously, my mother began to fade from involvement with me when I was seven years old. I bore this in silence as no explanation was offered. I also felt inhibited from asking about it, sensing my questioning wasn't an option. This was a painful and confusing time as I ached with longing, and emotional desolation. Within two years, my mother, whom I utterly depended upon for my very sustenance and survival, was dead--again without explanation or even acknowledgment of impact on me. No emotional support was offered. Not a word was said. It seemed that the agreed upon way of managing this catastrophe was to remain silent about it. The madness of this is incomprehensible to me now but at nine years old, I was simply in a state of numbness and shock, too young to assess anything. The silence characterizing those years and beyond was devastating.

Now, Lichen's silent presence evokes this early unfathomable pain, and I must face its deep impact without the protective numbness of my childhood. My slowly emerging understanding of Lichen's call to me was for this very healing purpose. As a child I could not allow the depth of loss and grief to fully register, and my young psyche ingeniously buried the threat of annihilation that such truth would bring. No psychotherapy could overcome my psyche's impenetrable defense since feeling the reality of that grief would bring me too close to the earlier experience of impending annihilation.

Lichen found a way to lead me where I needed to go by first surrounding me with a sense of unitive Love. That Love became the vehicle for the treacherous inner work ahead, helping me stay the course.

I am challenged to learn to extricate my own history from the beauty that silence carries. Imagine living hundreds of years, descending from beings over the span of hundreds of millions of years, and never making a sound, at least not detectable by humans. No sound needed for this epic journey that began before ice ages and dinosaurs and continues still.

***

I am visiting Carlsbad Caverns in New Mexico, marveling at the underground world of water-sculpted contours and shapes only visible because of the electric lights dotting our path. Our guide asks the group to sit on a low wall and remain still and silent. After a brief warning about impending darkness, he switches off all artificial light and we are left in total blackness. He suggests we put one of our hands directly in front of our faces so that we can "see" what true darkness is with our eyes open. At that underground depth, we are completely shielded from any daylight and cannot discern the edges of our hands despite having open eyes. Simultaneously we experience utter silence, at least until someone's breathing becomes faintly audible.

This is my first opportunity to sit within such a combination of absolute darkness and silence in the presence of other people. Although this moment is relatively fleeting, the impact is clear. I experience a sense of deep serenity and well-being coupled with profound reverence. Eventually I hear whispers and movements as others around me apparently become uncomfortable or restless with this out of the ordinary state of being. My grief is almost immediate as I know this rare opportunity has slipped away.

"It is through your experience of the indifference of my profound silence and stillness, well beyond the capacity of humans for either of those states, that can lead you to greater consciousness." **Lichen**

INDIFFERENCE

Indifference is clean

purely mirroring
the depths

There is neither deflection
nor target for projection

No contamination
or manipulation

The truth of love
may emerge here

Wild and barren place
can teach this

as no other human will
or ever can

DESERT MONASTERY

Two years elapsed since my initial encounter with Lichen in the Ponderosa forest. I've anticipated this upcoming stay in the desert for several months now, often with apprehension or actual fear. My psyche senses something ominous ahead but I don't yet grasp what this is. I'm on the last travel segment, driving down a 13-mile stretch of unpaved, sandstone derived road. On my right are soaring red, yellow and white cliffs of eroded and carved sandstone; the colors are warm and evocative as the light accents the surfaces unevenly. Below are junipers, cholla cactus, and an endless expanse of sage. I stop to caress the sage, bringing the intoxicating aroma close to my nose. There are no other cars on this remote stretch, so I can stop whenever I choose and simply roam around, briefly leaving my car in the middle of the road. On my left is the Chama River, snaking its way and basking in the achievement of its relentless erosion of this valley. The juxtaposition of desert and full flowing river is stunning. The light is slightly diffuse, soft, due to moisture in the air in contrast to the pristine clarity I witnessed on my first visit here over a year ago.

I travel to this monastery to deepen conversation with Lichen and give voice to more of her teachings through writing in the silence of this place. I'm hopeful that Lichen will be present here, but I am beginning to worry. I previously spent five days farther south in New Mexico along the Rio Grande and did not see any Lichen; so far along this drive I still haven't encountered Lichen. My view is continuously drawn to the compelling and dramatic river valley on my left.

Eventually, I break the spell of the river and look away to my right. I'm delighted to see I'm in the middle of a community of granite boulders, all of which are covered in various species and colors of Lichen. I feel so exhilarated by this finding that I stop the car again, get out, and offer a respectful bow with words of gratitude. I then make my way through the cactus and sand to place both hands on the Lichen for a more direct expression of gratitude, including a gentle and reverent kiss. I believe I'm passing through a threshold, a portal offered by Lichen to invite me further in. For the remainder of the ride to the desert monastery, another eight miles, I do not see Lichen again and wonder if I will.

As I rest in my small monastic quarters, I scan the basic room. It has a single bed, a free-standing roughly hewn wood carved closet, a desk, and a nightstand. There are two small windows, one in the entry door and the other on the opposite wall behind the head of the bed. I decide to see if the wall window opens, which it does. As I look out, I see that I'm almost at ground level and off to the right Lichen is waiting on several stones. I feel this loving welcome and quickly leave the room for a greeting.

Oh my! The riches are overwhelming! I will be residing in a treasure trove of Lichen, intimately living on sandstone, juniper bark, sage stems, and even a trace on the seemingly inhospitable cholla.

My room is at the end of the guest quarter building immediately accessible to all of this right outside my door. The fragrance of sage, swirling juniper bark, red erosion dirt, waxy yellow blooms of cholla, and more, are all luxuriating below the towering richly colored cliffs above. In the opposite direction, the Chama River flows beyond a field of dry whitish yellow desert shrubs that play host to a herd of massive black cows meandering in and out of view. There are pines too; Lichen has found them and spreads Love on their trunks.

As I continue to take in my surroundings, I recall Lichen's call to me just last week as I was driving to New Mexico and ruminating about an annoying email. While my mind was chattering through irritations and devising clever, witty written responses to assert my mental superiority, I heard, *"Look at you! This is petty."* When I registered this, I reflexively heard myself say, *"Is that you, Lichen?"* Somehow, I had known that the *"Look at you!"* had not been a production of my own mind. This was when I first realized that Lichen was using my own thoughts and language to communicate with me. And so, I had called out, *"Is that you, Lichen?"* The next thing I heard was, *"Remember I came to you in Love."* I immediately stopped my previous egoic machinations and entered a state of calm gratitude. The first teaching had been delivered and I was awed.

I know that during my stay I'll need to continue to hold close these loving words, *"Remember, I came to you in Love,"* since it's likely I'll repeatedly be hijacked by mental ruminations. I know Lichen is teaching me, with some firmness, I might add, how to remain in the largest conversation, the language of Love. And now I seem to have arrived at the breast of Love itself among these desert beings all held in Lichen's loving embrace.

***

There is a photograph on the wall of my monastery guest house room. The image is a painting by William Adolphe-Bouguereau, a French painter of the late 19th and early 20th century. This particular painting, titled L'Innocence, was painted in 1893 and is a soft yet clear depiction of a young mother clothed in flowing white with an ivory gown and head shawl draped gently around her body. She is standing barefoot on the edge of a shallow stream near a forest and holding both a sleeping infant against her chest and a baby lamb whose gaze is directed distantly away. There is a written analysis accompanying this image, describing it as the Virgin Mary "bursting with love for her child." The lamb is seen as a portent of what is to come, namely the "sacrifice of the Lamb of God on the Cross." Despite this ominous future held in the image, the present moment is one of tender beauty and radiant maternal love. The idea is that such beauty and love prepare one for violent future storms while infusing a sense of well-being in the present.

In my own biography, I too was held with tender beauty and love while the future held devastating trauma and death. Like this painting offers, that very foundation of Love also sees me through the journey of this wound. Lichen has led me here to this desert, this monastery, to this particular room to gaze upon this potent image. I came here to write in the service of Lichen, and I am humbled by this divine path laid out for me one step at a time. The last lines of the interpretation of the painting are as follows:

> *"When you experience genuine beauty (and love) in any of its forms, you must recognize it for what it is: the truth. In doing so, you will be prepared for the violent storms of life, able to see beyond the chaos no matter how deeply dark the day appears. For in and behind it all, there is always a Mother, tenderly cradling you, her precious child."*

And so, with these uplifting words and the knowing that I am surrounded by Lichen just outside my door, I eat the remainder of my traveling food for dinner and settle for an early bedtime. I am not prepared for what comes next.

DARK NIGHT OF THE SOUL

What a night! Each time I begin to drift into sleep in my monastery cell, I awake gasping for air. This continues the entire night and I'm never able to cross the threshold into sleep without panic. It feels as though I will stop breathing if I don't consciously keep it going. In addition, my throat begins to ache and throb. I get up several different times to go outside to the common bathroom area in the complex. It is dark and the desert night is cold. I inch my way each time, for some reason not choosing to take a headlamp with me. After four such excursions rather than face the panic of trying to sleep, I have one brief moment of reprieve when I see that the clouds have cleared, and the stunning expanse of stars is visible. I am grateful the stars have been revealed since it distracts me from the hellish nature of the night. This only briefly comforts me however, as I must return to my room due to the cold and exhaustion I feel.

I assume the higher elevation here is at least partly the cause of my need to gasp for air, although this is puzzling since I am often at this elevation without such effect. I do recall having some breathing difficulties when camping at 16,000 feet on a mountain climb in Africa many years ago and one night at 9500 feet in Colorado, but the elevation here is only just above 6000 feet. I feel increasing desperation and fear and know I must leave here even though I had just begun to explore the land and feel Lichen's welcome outside my room.

My body is demanding that I leave even though I've been here less than 24 hours. I had planned this eight day stay for over two months, but now I cannot imagine risking another night like this. I'm in a state of terror. I organize and pack my few things, walk up the gravel road to get my car and drive it back to pack it. I'm oddly comforted by the blackness of the night through this process. I then drive to the monastery church and office to notify the guest master that I must leave. It is about 3:00 am but his assistant is there since church services start quite early here. I explain that I have developed some kind of illness, and he is compassionate. I then drive off to confront the 13 miles of dirt road in the darkness and seclusion. I regret leaving at night and missing the magnificent and compelling vistas I know surround me, but I feel I have no choice.

I drive all the way to Santa Fe, a little more than two hours, before dawn begins to break the darkness. Eventually with great effort, wrestling with fatigue and sleeplessness, I arrive in Amarillo, Texas. Even though it is only midday, I must stop and find a room to rest, hopefully to sleep at this lower elevation. I do rest, but again, cannot sleep, gasping for air at that threshold of dissolving consciousness. My throat is quite painful with each swallow, and I feel I'm in the throes of an epic battle, both physical and spiritual. I'm disappointed because I've now aborted both the eight-day silent writing stay in the desert monastery and a nature-based writing immersion program in Colorado that was to immediately follow.

In Amarillo, later that evening I still cannot cross the threshold into sleep even though I do not gasp quite as frequently. It seems that I am prohibited from sleep by an intensely raging war within me. One side is keeping me awake and the other is trying to pull me below into dream and shadow realms. Somehow, I know that Lichen is at the center of this conflagration within me but what is it all about? How will I come through this or will I?

It is Halloween and I am in my own horror story, denied sleep, facing the proximity of Death, and compelled to grope my way in the long hours of darkness in a state of exhaustion and depletion. Is this the journey Lichen wants for me? Is it my pathway to deeper understanding of this ancient one's half billion year old presence on this planet? I know I can't use my usual mental processes to grasp this and so must somehow give way to the flow of it. It seems I am meant to stay in this border state between wake and sleep rather than traverse the usual daily quick passage from one to the other and back again. That edge is being expanded and becoming a place for me to reside rather than pass through, yet I am fighting to retain the familiar and easy transition each night into sleep and each morning into wakefulness. Lichen is showing me something in this liminal place; I trust I will learn as I write this during yet another sleepless night.

I arrive home in my exhaustion. My pain "has me by the throat" and even swallowing water is difficult. Karen, my life partner, makes a broth for me, which soothes my throat and gives me respite. I then succumb to her recommendation of going to Urgent Care where I am diagnosed with Strep throat and prescribed the appropriate antibiotic plus numbing mouthwash to block the pain in my throat. (I later learn that the Usnea species of Lichen has been used as a remedy for Strep throat.) The physician surmises that my throat pain may be actually affecting some respiratory reflex that leads me to gasp as I drift off to sleep. Interesting theory but I doubt it has validity.

This night as I attempt to sleep, I try to open myself to a shift and settle in to falling asleep in the way I have always been able to do. But the panicked gasps continue to stop me each time sleep approaches. I finally get up and explore this curious and dismaying condition through Internet searching. I find others have written about similar maladies. Some accounts relate to neurologic disease, which alarms me. I'm disheartened as there seems to be no way out of it and I begin to envision a drastic alteration of my life, making my way from this point on essentially without adequate sleep. I keep exploring these symptoms on the Internet and find a disturbing description of something called Central Sleep Apnea. However, I gravitate to a more psychological etiology involving anxiety or stress, which sits better as an explanation even though I don't understand what's happening.

While feeling trapped in this unending bout of fear of dying if I were to sleep, I hear a voice again. The words are profound and penetrating: *"You must Love your way into your own Death."* I knew it was Lichen's voice because of both the centrality of Love in the teaching and the foreignness of the idea to my own way of thinking. Out of desperation, I'm willing to give it a try, *Loving my way into death* without really understanding how. I'm so exhausted and sleep deprived that I easily start to drift into sleep again. Again, the panic of stopping breathing soon re-emerges but this time I decide to let it happen and try to embrace my death if that is what is meant to be. I have a sense of letting go of life itself.

I'm soon aware that I have a brief moment of sleep while sitting up in my reading chair. The panic seems to subside in intensity, so I make my way to bed to try again. I lean or fall into the sense of impending Death through the acceptance that Love offers and let this permeate my entire body. I feel ready to accept my Death if that's what being asked of me...

My next awareness is that I have been sleeping several hours and I am both surprised and relieved!

***

The monastery experience remained a mystery to me for several months. Gradually I was able to review the process once I had enough distance from the sheer terror of it. The visit to the monastery occurred soon after multiple structures of my life had been dismantled. I had recently retired from professional work after 37 years and moved from a place I had lived for 27 years, returning to the land of my birth and childhood. Powerful repressed forces were finally breaking free of my carefully constructed achievement and responsibility-laden world, and I was now living in closer proximity to the place where my original childhood trauma occurred. That trauma was essentially about my numbing and wall-creating response to repel unfathomable grief. My psyche had sensed I was not capable of feeling it at that early age and did everything possible to protect me from psychological annihilation. I am grateful for that, but it was clearly not the end of the story.

As I approached the trip to the monastery, I experienced both anticipation and dread that I didn't understand. Now I see what I was fearing. Prior to that trip, my body gave me warning symptoms including vertigo, headaches, lightheadedness, and even the ophthalmic condition of posterior vitreous detachment. I now see that body language as telling me, "it's time to let it back in, the grief so long avoided." Apparently even prior to being at the monastery, walls in me were dissolving to create an opening for the image of that painting to penetrate me.

When I review the experience, "I felt as though my brain would not keep me breathing if I did not stay awake," I think that's another way of saying that my ego world of daylight was afraid to give way to the dark, unconscious, shadow world that harbors the frightening forces of grief, despair, despondency. These parts of me had been buried in shadow for 58 years and I needed to face and reintegrate them for deeper healing. Lichen helped guide me there. I was drawn to that monastery for the sole purpose of writing about Lichen. At least that's what I thought. Apparently, Lichen had a larger and more important plan for me.

LOVE YOUR WAY INTO YOUR OWN DEATH

At the monastery I was surrounded by Lichen, or in other words, surrounded by Love. In that context, although I felt the fear of dying, Love and Death became inextricably joined for me. This seeming paradox became reconciled as I, with Lichen's invitational guidance, "loved my way into the Death" I feared sleep would bring.

"Remember I came to you in Love" comes to me again as I review my time in the monastery. An afternoon discovering the Lichen treasure outside my room, the painting depicting a mother's exultant Love for her infant son amidst the natural world, and then the fear of dying if I were to succumb to sleep. I fled that place; was I so profoundly disturbed by the invitation of such Love waiting for me? Was that Love really my death? Are they the same for me? I eventually Loved my way into the fear of death and finally slept. This experience may be the essence of my purpose in this life—Love my way into Death. Loving myself into Death is the greatest teaching I have ever received. Surrounded by the love of Lichen outside and facing the original love of my mother before her death, I felt close to my own death if my ego did not remain vigilant—I did not trust I would survive through sleep and had to stay awake. But that was not truly "awake"— it was clinging to a "smaller" state of awareness before venturing into the greater one that surrender to Love and Death would bring.

"I came to you in Love," the profound offering of Lichen is now coming to me at even deeper levels. I am beginning to understand Love beyond my intellectual attempts to describe or delineate it. I was initially offered this teaching while still a child reckoning with death, but then it was an almost lethal, searing wound that my need for survival would not abide. Now, it is the enduring lesson of my life.

INTERSPECIES "MARRIAGE" AND INTERCONNECTION TRINITY

"In the beginning was relationship." In his book, *The Divine Dance,* Richard Rohr makes this emphatic proclamation. Perhaps the most radical insight any of us can have is this awesome awareness of the interconnectedness of everything in the cosmos. Without this awareness, we are surely on a self-destructive course. As scientific inquiry and investigative techniques develop in complexity and sophistication, the fundamental relationship that is the basis of all that we know, or don't know, becomes clearer. Science and spiritual discipline begin to converge rather than stubbornly adhere to opposing camps of warring, dismissing dogmas. Einstein's famous equation of light, mass, and energy is the most widely known distillation of this fundamental relationship, one that can be interpreted in Christian theological terms as the concept of Trinity. Light, the Father, Incarnation/mass, the Son, and Energy, the Holy Spirit that drives the relational process. And although "Father" and "Son" are masculine concepts, it is the feminine that holds all through relationship. Structure may be delineated in a masculine framework, but without the feminine energy there is no wholeness to creation. To eliminate the feminine from the Divine is to take a path of self-destruction as we can see in process now in Western culture.

Lichen, ancient holder of planetary wisdom, reveals this very Trinity in possibly a more accessible manifestation. The fungi create the structure, algae, within that protective fungal structure, gather photons of light and ultimately produce energy from the miraculous photosynthetic process, the original sustainable use of natural resources (the sun). And with recent discoveries there is a second, yeast-type fungus usually necessary for this being to successfully enact all of this transformative work. A trinity of seeming individuals that become one, altering the morphology that any of them held when previously separate. The Christian religious incantation, "Father, Son, and Holy Spirit," often robotically spoken while poorly grasped can be seen manifest in this tangible form all around us. Lichen, the original symbiotic being, brings the facets of the Trinity into one transformed and enduring Being carrying this profound teaching for us all to see.

The Christine Center in Willard, Wisconsin has adopted a beautiful daily blessing as a vehicle for understanding this Trinitarian relationship in slightly different language:

> *We are one mind in the Light of Holy Wisdom (the Father)*
> *We are one heart in the radiance of Pure Love (the Beloved Son)*
> *We are one body in the resonance of Divine Power (Holy Spirit)*
> *All of creation is one (interconnected)*

In light, love, and power—
As it was in the beginning, is now, and ever
shall be.

In order for fungi and algae to create a new being, Lichen, a particular achievement was necessary. One step in that process is that these partners had to overcome defenses against "otherness" to develop a stable relationship. What a teaching this is! It seems that the greatest obstacle in the establishment of stable, adaptable, and enduring human relations, whether between two individuals, or among groups or nations, is this very challenge: defenses and the view of the other as a "pathogen," dangerous in some way.

How did Lichen make this leap? Perhaps it took millions of years of gradual smaller steps of "risk taking" to settle in to such a radical transformation. This process seems to reveal the overarching fabric of Love in order for its success. It is a dying to the smaller structure in order to expand into the next. Love is the relational substrate of this proliferation of more complex and enduring life form, not division and "hatred" of the other. Nature has many examples of mutualistic collaboration between divergent species in order to assure each of their survival. Trees and mycorrhizal fungi are in continuous alliance underground along the root systems. The very energy that powers our cells is generated by former bacteria, now mitochondria, that are part of our basic cellular anatomy. We alter, grow, and endure because of relationship. As Richard Rohr so simply states, the

Trinity is the basic structure of the universe. At the atomic level of all that exists, there is a relationship component, an essential life energy, a fundamental attraction. This is a more expansive view of the concept of Eros.

Marriage has become a battleground for human rights. Should we be so limited as to reduce the essential meaning of marriage to a human arrangement? Perhaps marriage was defined for us long before we even existed as part of creation itself, the joining of two disparate beings, or as said in philosophy, reconciliation through the dialectic process of seemingly contradictory forms or forces.

As many people of Western cultural heritage steadfastly and righteously assert, marriage is "between a man and a woman." One has only to attend to the natural world, also created by Mystery (or God, depending on your preferred orientation) to see beyond this anthropomorphic confine. Clearly that narrow view underscores the sense of separation from the natural world inherent in this dominant culture and provides fodder for deep rifts and persecution.

Lichen may be the first long-lasting marriage on the planet and as such provides a model for all of us. It is a union in which multiple individuals retain their unique gifts yet create an entity of deep "we-" or "us-" ness, not classifiable as either of its individual parts. Fungi and algae (or cyanobacteria), while quite different biologically, somehow found each other and were open to the possibilities despite their profound differences.

This is not an ephemeral connection or brief "romance." The involvement is not based on mere tolerance of diverse difference but instead a deep interplay resulting in structural changes. Tolerance, a word frequently used to help facilitate coexistence of different human ethnicities, religious groups, races, genders, sexual orientation, etc., misses the mark. It implies continued separation and suppression of lurking irritations or hostilities kept under wraps. Settling for mere "tolerance" deprives us of the rich, transformative alterations that can occur with true interplay and actual melding of such diverse differences.

Lichen is not a plant, not a fungus, not an alga but a creative admixture, an awesome validation of life's energetic possibilities. The evolutionary achievement represented by Lichen can serve as a model for how we conceptualize the gift of diversity offered to us within our own human range. Lichen's internal relationship of its parts allows each foundational individual to survive in a transformed state when conditions would be otherwise incompatible with ongoing life for either alone. Cyanobacteria and alga are the earliest beings to weave light and carbon dioxide in air (photosynthesize) into food energy (sugars), but in harsh, challenging conditions, need a structurally protective home to work this magic. Certain fungi have become quite hospitable (maybe at times somewhat exploitative, but that's another line of exploration), opening their homes, even at the microscopic level to welcome these creative beings in. Not only do the fungi provide a safe haven to collect moisture and shield from the drying effects of sun, but they also extract needed minerals from the surrounding environment to augment the algal or cyanobacterial production of energy. Such is the enduring marriage of Lichen, built on essential needs and complementary labors.

Once this marriage has formed, the challenge of procreation is now paramount. How else can the living system continue to flourish and create new possibilities? Clearly humans need gametes to connect for this to occur but a marriage between a "man" and a "woman" is only one option in a much larger system in which gender is on a continuum rather than dualistically separated. Socio-culturally, there are numerous variations both in procreation and child rearing. Direct sexual intercourse, in-vitro fertilization, in-utero insemination, and surrogacy offer creative ways to continue the legacy and evolution of humanity.

When a human community functions in harmony with the self-organizing and fluid character of the larger wild living system within which it emerged, there is no place for the pursuit of disconnection from and exploitation of the natural world, the creation of illusory categories of hierarchy, or rigid gender boundaries. Examples of procreative variation abound in the wild and should serve as our guide. Even within the realm of Lichen itself, there are several possibilities for the creation of "offspring." Both sexual and asexual reproduction occur.

Photosynthesis is one of the supreme achievements of life on earth. But as the animal kingdom further evolved, this capacity for directly transforming photons of light into sustenance was lost. As a result, most all faunae must rely on those beings who continue to have this energy and oxygen producing ability. And so those with photosynthetic capacity provide the gift of life for all of us supposedly "more complex" creatures who are decidedly lacking in such self-reliance.

Clearly, we are not necessary for these beings to flourish as indeed they did for eons before our appearance. There is no greater gift than what these beings offer us. Each breath we take and every other energy dependent activity within us arises from this gift. At the least, these miraculous beings merit our reverence, devotion, gratitude, and stewardship.

It appears that the only remnant of solar energy transformation that we humans can claim comes through Vitamin D production when skin is exposed to sunlight. Vitamin D has a direct relationship to the absorption of calcium needed to create and maintain our skeletal structure in addition to its possible connection to other system processes, immunity enhancement, and disease prevention. In this circuitous way of using light, one might say we continue the marriage of energy and structure founded by algae and Lichen eons ago.

Humans take in the energy created through photosynthesis through eating plants or other animals who in turn have ingested plants, absorb ultraviolet light through the skin to produce Vitamin D, and through a complex series of biochemical processes, develop the bone based structure needed for protection, support, and movement. Although this is an elaborate and sophisticated achievement, the simpler and more basic union of energy and mass so exquisitely found in Lichen seems closer to the original, incarnation of spirit into matter at the dawn of creation of living systems on this planet.

The capacity to risk relinquishing one's familiar structure and routine without either understanding or certainty of where this will lead is the essence of faith. Faith in the inherent "benevolence" of the cosmic flow, not in an unproven belief of some kind. This is an act of Love, quite different from making choices designed to control, achieve, assure security, or give rise to hierarchy. It is the embracing of Love as the primary force and container of the cosmos, a willingness to risk the vulnerability of loss of ego control and flow into a mysterious and unpredictable realm. The investment in the illusion of separation becomes obsolete and connection to vast, limitless cosmic energy then sustains the journey.

Lichen's pioneering achievement of symbiosis which has given it superpowers of longevity and enduring presence on the planet beyond most other organisms has challenged previously held scientific notions that organisms must compete for survival. Collaboration as seen in Lichen, was not recognized in the evolutionary theories of the late 19th 20th century.

Their symbiotic nature also challenges our concept of what entails an autonomous being, an individual. As Merlin Sheldrake writes in *Entangled Life: How Fungi Make Our Worlds, Change Our Minds, and Shape our Futures:*

> *Lichens are living riddles. Since the 19th century, they have provoked fierce debate about what constitutes an autonomous individual. The closer we get to lichens, the stranger they seem. To this day, lichens confuse our concept of identity and force us to question where one organism stops, and another begins.*

My relationship with Lichen has taught me the power of interspecies connection beyond the relatively superficial levels of mere observation, scientific exploration, or phylogenetic categorization. Within this unexpected and deeply foreign "marriage," I've been guided into challenging realms, through core psychological wounds into a paradigm changing comprehension of the interconnectedness of all phenomena on this planet and even beyond. I've had to wrestle with basic elements of human suffering: aloneness, the construction of linear time, the vacuum of silence and stillness, fear of death, separation from reality, and the collapse of numerous ego-generated illusions.

It is in fact because of the vast differences between Lichen and my humanness, that I've been propelled into this uncharted course. There is no refuge in sameness here except in our shared reliance on the overarching living system of the Earth for ongoing survival. Essentially, I can take nothing for granted in this relationship. We do not pursue similar interests yet continue to maintain relationship. Or at least I do. I realize that Lichen has served as a portal for me into awareness of the interconnectedness of all phenomena and truly is not confined to connection with me specifically.

This is a hard teaching to hold since I tend to repeatedly resort to the limitations of human pursuits of Love that are usually restricted to individual relationships rather than cosmic interconnection. It is Lichen's seeming detachment from or indifference to me that keeps the teaching of Love going at a cosmic level.

This has not been a smooth journey, despite Love being the guide. There has been profound disruption and even terror along the way. Had I not been invited through an initial experience of profound loving envelopment, I would not have traveled this often perilous route. It seems that such a cosmic sense of Love is irresistible, dissolving even the most intense longings that likely begin at human birth. Longings bring disconnection from present reality but even brief periods of inhabiting the realm of cosmic Love lights the way for greater awareness of reality. Consciousness

expands and despite its elusiveness can never fully
return to the previous level of constriction.

55

Dear Lichen,

After months of separation from you, I am finally making contact. I spoke with you two days ago while sitting on the tree stump where you live in the backyard. I confessed to you that I have felt negligent or guilty even though I have not forgotten what you have given me and continue to lead me into. It's been such a profoundly challenging journey for me. Love is the only way I would have taken the first step. It's interesting now that I write that I'm recalling the analysis of the L'Innocence painting at the monastery. It emphasized the foundation of Love as the holder for future pain, the portent of death in the form of the sacrificial lamb. This is how my life began. I was born into Love. I then faced the devastation of death, which disrupted me to my core. I have been "wholing" and healing ever since. That day in May, three years ago, you invited me back. You offered me an intoxicating, enveloping, almost womblike new beginning for me to travel that pathway of Love and Death again. It is the journey of my life and I live in the awe of it.

During our meeting, after you called and lovingly abducted me in the northern New Mexico pine forest, I was so sure of the Love that I unambivalently entered into a marriage vow with you. The reverence was encompassing and as I walked away, back into my culture, there was a gravity I felt that slowed my pace and rooted me deeply to the earth. This was a critical time, a shift in everything, a re-entry into myself. That time with you was transcendent as I believe cosmic love is. After that, my journey has been inscendent, inward, as Bill Plotkin and others have named. Your Love has given me faith in the journey that I had put aside for decades. What I have learned has much to do with feeling grief fully, an equal and inextricable facet of Love. They are not really separate for me. This is the wisdom you have brought me and the Grace of this is ineffable.

I will close this letter now. There is much more to say.

I am finding my Voice and sharing it with you as I listen deeply to your voice emerging within me.

Lover of Lichen

HEALING

THE HEALING

A significant amount of time, at least in human scale, passed before I began to understand the healing gift of the mysterious journey that Lichen has guided me on. What I previously ignored or noticed only peripherally, became the holder of the deepest healing force I have yet to know. This itself is a teaching of great consequence. Outside the margins of our attention and beyond the familiar frameworks of perception profound gifts await. Our routines and habits, comfortable belief systems, and culturally promoted goals often blind us to what would likely benefit us most.

We all carry wounds, some less visible than others, and without bringing them to the light of consciousness, these wounds continue to orchestrate our choices and obscure our wisest discernment abilities. Because these wounds are such tender and vulnerable aspects of our psyches, often indicative of early traumas, we are unwittingly protected from knowing them fully. Our young psyches brilliantly guard us from immersion in this realm, sensing danger or annihilation if these responses to trauma were to overtake us.

The painting I saw in the monastery cell, L'Innocence, by William Bouguereau, is key to understanding the healing part of my journey with Lichen. I had been guided to that monastery ostensibly to write about Lichen. Encountering the painting seemed incidental, another peripheral meeting like my initial experience with Lichen had been. The image itself penetrated a half century of psychic protection through surprise and immediacy. There was no defense. This image captured the essence of my childhood wound in a flash. I didn't register this at the time. Later that night, I faced my impending death, feeling in my body that my breathing would cease if I did not remain awake and vigilant. This prevented me from sleeping for three consecutive nights with no sense that it would ever end. It seemed my death was inevitable without an understandable cause. Puzzling, mysterious, inexplicable, and terrifying.

My childhood history solves this powerful mystery, but it took months for me to see it. When I was nine years old, in fourth grade, I was called to the principal's office by an announcement over the public address system used in those days. I walked alone, bewildered, down the long corridor of the school to reach the office. When I arrived, two older women were standing there in front of the principal's desk. I did not recognize them; they were total strangers to me. I can still remember their flower printed silk-like dresses that seemed to hiss when they moved. Even though they were strangers to me, the principal authorized them to take me out of the building, telling me they were driving me home.

I sat in the backseat while they both were in front. As we turned out of the school driveway onto the street, the woman in the passenger seat turned to me and said, "your mother passed away." Immediately, I felt as if I had been struck by lightning in the center of my chest, leaving a deep hole. I also felt like I was no longer there. Because of my silence, that same woman asked me if I knew what "passed away" meant. I remember my thoughts in that moment: "Passed out means fainting so passed away means dead." I mustered a frail response. "Yes," I whispered. Not another word was spoken.

When I arrived at my house it was full of people, some of whom I recognized as friends of my parents. They were milling around in our living room holding drinks. One woman rumpled my hair and said, "Isn't he cute!" Another person said something like, "You can play at our house anytime." I didn't know either of them.

I was in a daze but eventually made my way back to my parent's bedroom. My father and older brother were there with a few other people. I remember my 17 year-old brother's contorted face as he was pacing in the room. My father was sitting on the edge of the bed and although he did embrace me, he said nothing. In fact, from that point on, no one ever said a word about my mother to me. I didn't find out why she died until four years later when a non-family member told me about her breast cancer.

On that car ride home from school, my psyche had protected me from an inconceivable truth. I simply could not have survived psychically if I had truly felt the devastation fully. My mother was my sustenance, and to a large degree my life depended on her. How could a nine year old face the reality of this? I did not have the capacity to understand and integrate it and without any emotional support or communication from others I was left severed from myself and certainly from the ability to feel grief. In retrospect I have realized it was too dangerous to feel anything. An additional horrific layer developed. There was something terribly wrong with me. No other child in my social or school world had a mother that died so I carried the feeling that I was responsible in some way, that I was terribly dangerous, even murderous. No one told me otherwise. All of these elements barricaded me from experiencing the grief I needed to feel.

In college, I decided to go to medical school for two main reasons. My mother had disappeared in some hidden medical world I had been prohibited from entering as a child. I wanted access to that. Also, I had a vague sense that she had revered doctors. Her brother was a physician as was her cousin, the doctor who delivered me. Since no one spoke of her to me after she died, I tried to hold on to anything I knew about her, and becoming a doctor was one way to stay connected to her.

I was also drawn to anything psychological, trying to understand what happened to me and find a way to heal myself. Psychiatry held the most appeal as other fields of medicine seemed too disconnected from what

I was after. I learned about psychopathology and was intrigued by that realm of study. I completed medical school and residency training by age 29 so by early adulthood I was seeing my own patients. I also entered psychotherapy myself.

Although I made some inroads into understanding various aspects of my own psychological story, I never truly experienced anything transformative in that process. I even went into psychoanalytic training and saw a psychoanalyst four days a week for several years. I played at feeling grief, but it was always contrived, never visceral. I knew I was a prisoner in some way but couldn't seem to find my way into a larger realm beyond those psychic confines.

My encounter with Lichen in that Northern New Mexico Ponderosa pine forest opened an unexpected and ultimately healing path for me. I was lured into this journey by the mystical Love infused experience that I've already described. This extraordinary encounter eventually led me to the painting in the monastery, a single image holding Love and Death. It is my story. A radiant mother cherishing her innocent son while simultaneously holding a lamb that portends death. In my case, it would be her own death and I will fall from this loving grace. The grief is beyond this innocent child's psychic capacity to feel and keep living and is therefore buried.

Seeing this image brought me into contact with the annihilation I had so long been shielded from by numbness. My body had held this wound in the center of my chest, where the news of my mother's death had initially struck me like a lightning bolt. For over a decade I actually experienced a sensation of a hole in my chest, invisible yet painfully palpable to me. It seems no accident that I was drawn to Lichen by an irresistible magnetic pull focused on that same part of my body. I now see that as the beginning of my healing at the body level, where my breathing emerges. The painting penetrated to the core of this woundedness, and my breathing became tenuous, no longer automatic. I felt I would die if I didn't stay awake and vigilant.

And so, I eventually learn from Lichen, "*you must Love your way into your own Death.*" I listened to this profound teaching and chose not only to allow my death but also welcome it with a loving embrace. I was then blessed with sleep from which I woke with a profound sense of healing and gratitude. After 58 years, Lichen had led me here and I am awed by this revitalizing gift.

My loving Lichen,

It has been over six weeks since I've written to you. Today it is time—I feel called to you as I feel the high tide of grief again. I am ready for the submersion as I know I must access more loss. I believe you as an emissary of Mystery and now it is time for me to let go of trying to change things, trying to keep, hold static, that which has been so enlivening and healing. But that energy has receded like the tide moving away. Now is the high tide of grief. I am in my own Bay of Fundy with grief towering over me as I stand on the place that receding magic energy has left bare. I feel bereft and my body is full, pressured from the inside to let grief flow. I have glimmers of what being present might look or feel like now; I see or witness myself anguished about the way it once was, longing for its return, despairing and hopeless that it will not, and fearful about where I go next. None of that is being present— this moment holds none of those elements. This moment is breath, light, interconnectedness, not all those other mental fabrications. You have lived so long I wonder how you experience me. Perhaps you don't— indifference may be the most accurate characterization of your involvement with me. Maybe you invited me into the web and then went on living. The rest is up to me I know. You planted the seed of powerful, encompassing Love—and the painting you led me to see in New Mexico mirrored what I must learn about such Love. I travelled through ego protection using Love as my guide into Death if that's where I must be taken.

It seems I may be heading toward another similar journey. My ego is clinging, like a child about to be torn away from his mother, not knowing where else to be or even if survival will continue to be possible. This is what is happening again and what I learned before is to Love my way into it in order for the next door to open into the unknown. I do have faith in this process, but I don't go easily or even willingly. Whether I protest or not, the path will pull me along. I hope I am beginning to lean into it and not dig my heels in and grasp to hold on, keep from moving along. I did this when moving from Little Rock to Dallas and once arriving in Dallas, becoming depressed, isolated, heading toward suicidality—13 years old and deeply pained and alone. This is an early grief that I must revisit so I suppose it's time to go there again, deeper. I thought I had gone through this already, but I realize I truly had not. Instead, I had intermittent reprieves that don't work anymore and actually don't even happen again. I'm reeling of the edge of grief, but I do welcome it. This is the only way through. Can I swim through it, across it, and still breathe? Where will I be? Whom will I be with, if anyone? My dear Lichen—I trust you will still be there.

In love and grief,
LL

GRIEF

A dark foreboding pool
ominously beckons
I know I must immerse

but hesitate

Choosing
anguish over grief

The pool is opaque
thick and viscous
Will I survive this
airless submersion
and breathe again?

It seems not, yet
I sense another place waits
if only I can brave the
Dissolving,
the Spasms
the gut twisting heaves

And give myself over
to the power
and swim through
the Grief

into Love

I'm walking a labyrinth—this one has borders of limestone roughly two inches thick balanced upright on their lower edges. The top edges are intermittently jagged or smooth and the stones themselves rise up to two feet making this a relatively deep labyrinth, a spiraling valley snaking through a diminutive, curved mountain range. I can imagine myself in miniature making my way, unable to see over these mountain-like stones. This metamorphosis allows me to be more fully present, deep within the maze and unable to plan ahead. I cannot see where I'm going but must have faith in the process, in the movement and in the space. I know I will safely arrive somewhere or is arrival even relevant?

The ground I walk upon is a natural soil pathway occasionally strewn with smaller stones, twigs, pine needles, and leaves. Many have come before me through these sentinel limestone walls. It is a lovely journey but what stuns me and leaves me momentarily breathless is the cover of Lichen that has found its place on almost every one of the hundreds of limestone fragments guiding me. The textures, colors, and patterns of this array of lichens seem infinitely variable and seeing this extensive blended family in such concentration and proximity to each other is lovely. I am surrounded every step of the way, enveloped by this ancient being and repeatedly reminded along every curve that I am home.

Only a few months earlier, I actually did return to this region where I was born, my original home. As a young adolescent I had been forced to leave this land against my will and in adapting to that loss, subsequently moved numerous times around the country, rootless. Now, more than half a century later, wounds no longer gaping, I venture back to this land of great natural beauty, where deciduous forests mixed with pine and cedar are dense, where cypress grow in shallow ponds, where rivers always have water flowing, where quartz abounds, and where billion year old diamonds can be discovered on the surface of earth's crust.

When I encountered Lichen in New Mexico years before, I had not immediately realized the pervasive gift inherent in that union. Unlike most other beings limited to certain habitats or climates, Lichen is essentially ubiquitous and never far from view in any natural setting. This is a great gift for me since I am welcomed everywhere by Lichen and feel at home as a result. This sense of belonging no matter where I wander is deeply soothing, even healing, and helps keep my awareness of interconnectedness fresh and active. I'm grateful for this effective antidote to the constant cultural pull toward separation, fragmentation, and isolation. I see myself belonging everywhere; I am home wherever I find Lichen and with the patience so central to true Love, it is always there waiting for me to reconnect, to welcome me home.

As I spiral inward, having let go of the need to reach a destination, I do in fact arrive at the labyrinth's center where I find something unexpected greeting me. A sculpted human form about half life-size stands facing me, arms slightly forward to bring hands together, palm to palm in a gesture of humble, supplicatory gratitude. I offer a slight bow in recognition, sharing this state of thankfulness. Gratitude truly resides at the center from which Love radiates.

SCORPION AND BETRAYAL

Over two years ago I had a dream with Scorpion as a prominent presence. Since then, I've been exploring my visceral aversion to these creatures while also holding some awareness of simultaneous allurement. During a five-day stay in the desert at Joshua Tree National Park, I shared my fear of Scorpion with someone who asked me what kind of fear it was. Without thinking I quickly blurted out, "Betrayal" and surprised myself.

This epiphany opened a door into a productive journey for me. The wound I was dealt when I had to face the death of my mother during my childhood was brought forth in a new perspective, with an added dimension. Yes, her death hurt deeply, almost beyond bearing, but it was the absence of her goodbye to me, the omission of any gift for preparation or acknowledgment of cherished connection (she knew she was dying of cancer) to help me weather the devastation ahead. This held the sting of Betrayal. And the Scorpion can look you eye to eye and sting you from above, essentially out of eye contact. Other creatures either bite while facing you or sting when facing away from you. Scorpions are different in this regard and seem almost diabolical when they inflict the sting in this unique way. This captures the experience that my mother, a source of unquestionable love until then, inadvertently left me with a deep betrayal delivered from the same source of original life-giving and nurturing love. She had faced me daily and never divulged the devastating almost lethal sting she knew was coming to me with her impending death. Betrayal! Life as I once knew it ended and I remember at nine saying to myself: "your childhood is over."

Daniel Deardorff writes in *The Other Within: The Genius of Deformity in Myth, Culture & Psyche*

> *"Betrayal--to be traded, delivered, handed over, no longer held, dropped--is the crisis of a rupture in the veil of the ordinary-life. A violation in which we are in-formed by assault: dis-possession, disappointment, dis-ease; every indignity, every wound, every curse, every tragic fall brings us to this crossroads."*

Deardorff goes on to say*:*

> *The betrayal of the promised life throws the broken and oppressed one down to the crossroads into the abyss: the famous "dark night of the soul."*

It was this crossroads that I revisited at the monastery when I was delivered into my own "dark night of the soul."

Betrayal, either through the act itself or the experience of its wound, precipitates a feeling of separation from the fabric of cosmic Love. In states of separation or isolation, beings often do not survive harsh conditions. Lichen is the outcome of organisms finding their way into connection, deeply holding each other, so deeply in fact that neither (and now there is evidence of a third symbiont) is left the same without sacrifice of their original essence. When I came upon Lichen and was invited into the presence of cosmic Love from this ancient, evolutionary ancestor, I began to feel the healing force of that Love at a profound level. Lichen knows about such Love and the power of transcending separation though its symbiotic achievement.

Lichen,

This wound journey you've lovingly deepened for me is opening me, expanding me, and I hope centering me into the seeds of elderhood. I have learned through this journey that woundedness is the buried treasure, a multifaceted gem that requires repeated visits through life's time course. The change in perspective over time determines which facet of the gem is brought to light. With each experiential visit, wholeness is gifted and ultimately there is a deepening of one's capacity to contribute to the healing of the cosmic whole.

Allowing—no, loving,--grief's delicious washing, cleansing, is sinking me deeper into the connection of belonging. This whole process is self-organizing and nourishing. I know I have been closed off to this, at least at the present level, for over half a century of man-measured time. As I write that, I'm awed by many things: the collapse of time, the enduring force of the cosmos to heal, to make whole, and most essentially, the fabric of Love that holds it all. Love is relational, Trinitarian by your living example. Life, Love, Energy...all interplaying—death is part of it all too.

Grieving is a form of loving expressed in response to life altering loss. Numbness produced through the shock of such devastating loss seems to seal grief inside the body. Apparently, we can't think our way into the release of this trapped grief despite all we learn about it. I intuitively knew that I needed the full expression of this body-centered emotion since childhood, but I have detoured frequently, finding it easier and more accessible to cultivate sexual body feeling to the exclusion of a fuller emotional body life. I am also learning that grief comes in waves. Perhaps these waves are as certain as the tides; maybe the unrelenting pull of Moon is connected. Women are pro-creatively connected to this lunar cycle. Maybe men are also resonating in this cycle but less clearly. I recall the total eclipse last summer when I realized the shadows cast by the moon-blocked sun, were spherical, not obliterated by usual sunlight since that dominant light source was relegated to a subservient place behind. It was a chance for a powerful experience of the dark, mysterious feminine to take ascendency. It was not lost on me and has only deepened my exploration into the masculine/feminine continuum. Not only in the culture but also within myself.

Of course this is central to the name of my core wound, a deep terror of the danger of the feminine love-betrayal dynamic, and a repression of the even more feared "murderous" masculine energy.

Lichen, my beloved, you came to me in Love, brought me to you in Love, led me to terror within with Love, and helped me realize my way through is with Love.

Love,
LL

WAITING

"Time is not the measure of anything important; don't revolve around it. Hurriedness is a choice of disconnection from the web of life. The flow is the speed to travel—don't impose an engine upon it to speed through or against it." **Lichen**

A being that has inhabited this planet for half a billion years, maybe even longer, certainly knows something about time. Perhaps enough to dispense with it altogether as any kind of constraint or tyrant to be obeyed or worshipped. I am listening to this teaching and beginning to realize the profound shift in consciousness that would emerge as a result of fully living into it.

Time is the measure of my days and my nights; I wore a watch for much of my life and more recently carry a smartphone so that I am never out of time's reach. I am on time's leash. I seek responses to almost everything I do, which means I am aware of the time until such response comes. I write emails and wait for response. I leave voice mail messages and wait for response. I speak to others and wait for response. And I don't like waiting.

But what if the waiting were to hold more for me than the response? What if I savored that space and began to experience the response as only a marker until I could inhabit the waiting space again? What could I experience if I were to love the waiting, rather than experience it as an irritation at best or a trigger for re-experiencing deep childhood wounds at its worst. Has Lichen been patiently waiting for me to ask this question? Actually "patience" is not a meaningful state to attribute to Lichen, not only because it is an anthropomorphic concept, but also because it is simply irrelevant to Lichen. It implies its opposite must also be held and Lichen is certainly not on the continuum of patience at one pole and impatience at the other. Lichen holds through such vast geologic time periods that it is not bound by the increments of time measurement that so thoroughly shape our human lives. We are brief creatures and although compared to most insects we seem to have a "long" lifespan, in truth we don't. What seems to differentiate us is our attempt to control time, to deny impermanence, prevent aging, and even try to outwit death. Without doing any of these things, Lichen endures well beyond the confines of human existence. Apparently, our so-called superior intelligence is but another delusion that humanity holds, delusional because human intelligence does not ensure our survival beyond that of a "lowly" being such as Lichen. And certainly, Lichen tells us by its very nature, that deep connection to the web of life rather than attempting to control it is key to enduring survival. Will our so-called superior intelligence measure up in comparison?

Our measurement and use of time creates inherent problems for us. Rather than dissolve time as Lichen teaches, we fight it as we seek to diminish or even eradicate waiting periods. Those periods seem to burden so many of us and even threaten us with the emergence of anxiety and fear. In response, we devise various "timesaving" methods and devices. Perhaps a more apt phrase would be "wait-reduction" rather than "timesaving." Although saving time could result in more opportunities for empty periods, we really don't want to save time so that we can have more waiting! Our culture creates more and more things to do so that waiting spaces are eliminated.

Jason Farman on waiting in *Delayed Response: The Art of Waiting from the Ancient to the Instant World:*

> *Waiting isn't an in-between time. Instead, this often hated and underappreciated time has been a silent force that has shaped our social interactions. Waiting isn't a hurdle keeping us from intimacy and from living our lives to our fullest. Instead, waiting is essential to how we connect as humans through the messages we send. Waiting shapes our social lives in many ways, and waiting is something that can benefit us. Waiting can be fruitful. If we lose it, we will lose the ways that waiting shapes vital elements of our lives like social intimacy, the production of knowledge, and the creative practices that depend on the gaps formed by waiting.*

If I seek to decrease the waiting gap or even leap over it completely, I am shaped by a future that is always out of reach. When I continuously ignore the present in which all treasure lies, I deplete myself and all beings that come in contact with me. No relational depth develops in this process of seeking the future.

When I say "beings" I mean all of creation that surrounds and permeates me. Not just what this dominant Western culture sees as animate, but all that is incarnated energy, from atom to stone, alga to whale, river to wind, light to darkness. All of these are beings, and, in that sense, all is animate. In Potawatomi culture and language, the term inanimate is reserved for human created objects only. I have adopted that perspective because it rings true to me.

***

Lichen has watched my foolhardy and desecrating traipse through the present, perhaps well before I was aware of this being. When I scan my photographs pre-dating by years my pivotal encounter with Lichen in that northern New Mexico Ponderosa pine forest, I often see Lichen as the featured subject. I was drawn even at those times to this being, so unlike the rest of the landscape. Although at those times my camera buffered me from direct relationship, I now imagine my presence was not lost on Lichen.

Years have little or no effect on Lichen since she flows at the rate of the planet herself. When the "time" was right, when there was a sense that I was ready and open, the invitation came. It was one of Love, irresistible and all-encompassing Love, the essence and fabric of this cosmos. My resistance was not possible or even sought. Lichen knew with an intelligence I can't fathom, that it was my time to meet her, that I could live through such an introduction to cosmic Love.

Lichen agreed through her membership in the web of life to serve as a portal for me and then called me in a language I had never known before. It came as I was in a state of presence. I could call that a period of "waiting" although at that moment I wasn't aware of waiting for anything in particular. I was lying down in a low expanse of small plants that covered the floor of a clearing. These generous beings had offered themselves as a carpet for me to rest on and attend to the industrious bees that visited the white flowers these small plants sported around my head and body. From that place of repose and stillness, the invitation came. If I had not been still and present, I would not have "heard" it. It was the gap in doing anything future directed that allowed me to receive that invitation. It was all in the presence of "waiting."

I'm making a pact with myself. I want to keep track of each time I am looking for a response of any kind. When I note this, I hope to detach from that seeking and truly see and be in relationship with all that holds me where I am now. I want to reciprocate, not just be an observer. I want to respond to what is, rather than look toward an external response. How liberating that might be! So much energy is squandered in this response seeking future orientation.

Lichen has showed me how to be in light, in dark, in all manner of climate change, in the full range of nutrient offering from abundance to nothing. One end of any spectrum is not superior to the other. A nourishment induced growth state is no more important than a period of energy suspension and closeness to death.

In fact, the different life forms that come together to generate the Lichen symbiosis hold these polar opposites. Algae or cyanobacteria are photosynthetic, energy generating, life creating beings, whereas fungi work in the realm of death, creating decay and degeneration. The symbiotic joining of these two disparate aspects, Life and Death, may be the deepest teaching of all.

Lichen remains intimately in relationship to what is, in whatever form the larger web is offering. It has survived multiple species extinctions on the planet and certainly may survive human extinction. But of course, the destructive power of radioactivity created by humans may actually affect Lichen, too. It has never encountered such an enduring poison that can persist for billions of years.

***

What would it mean to fully inhabit the waiting state? How could I learn the balance of waiting and action? Could I discern when it is optimal to live into waiting or to engineer some movement toward a future state? Is it possible to trust the flow so fully that I could simply let everything unfold with that as guide? When I imagine doing that, the concept of waiting actually evaporates since there is continual impermanence in all that is, even in Lichen's realm.

If I were to focus on the power of waiting in human relationships rather than response, how would those relationships unfold? I know it would be a different process than what I usually, or maybe always am engaged in. It's a shift from relying on and believing in the importance of plans constructed by my ego to a deep faith in the larger web of Mystery as guide. Until now, I have not grappled with this concept, at least not in a sustained way, and I'm wondering if my outcome seeking ego has been part of the flow all along. Perhaps I had to swim in that before I could approach the cascade that I would plummet over into a different paradigm. Certainly not a "fall" I would willingly enter.

Early this morning, I was given this dream:

> *I am sent out on a wander as part of some intensive workshop for my psyche. There are other people there. I start to climb a grassy hill with initial doubt about my physical endurance but then feel some strength and capability in the ascent. When I reach the top, I turn to my*

left and start moving downhill, walking. The terrain has changed to stones without green and I start to experiment with a skating motion by moving my feet over the smooth stones. Eventually I am able to slide without individual skate movements, like I am skiing in my shoes with my feet held together (as in parallel skiing) over the stones. I gain speed and feel some exhilaration, freedom, and joy. Soon I see a ravine not too distant from me. I keep going with a sense of being able to manage this upcoming drop-off. I do in fact sail off the edge but while I am mid-air see that my landing will likely be beyond my capacity to survive. Fear! Before I hit the bottom, I awake.

I'm struck by the changes in my feeling states in this dream. I begin with doubt, develop some sense of competency, move into a sense of exhilaration, freedom, and joy, sense potential danger without initial fear, and then awake in a moment of terror. Is this the terrain I am facing as I move more deeply into Waiting? Is there a death ahead for me? It certainly seems yet another ego death is coming. Holding out for the reprieve of responses may have been serving me in this way, helping me postpone this next death I must face. I've been led here by awakening to witnessing my response seeking rather than being blindly immersed in it. I've also been helped along the way by those who do not respond as I wish and therefore do not collude with this attempted refuge.

We live in an instantaneous culture. Most everything we want to know is available quickly and we have the capacity to communicate immediately with almost anyone on the planet. And we expect results. The more tech savvy one is, the more competent. Those of us who lag behind the latest innovation are seen as less "with-it" which can easily translate into less intelligent. Certainly not holders of any valuable wisdom. Immediacy is worshipped, and a slower, flowing process is denigrated.

Bill Plotkin in his writings, particularly *Wild Mind: A Field Guide to the Human Psyche*, describes four windows of knowing, which he attributes to Elegio Stephen Gallegos' work. Two of them, thinking and perception through our senses, are recognized and validated by our culture to varying degrees, but the other two, full-bodied feeling and imagining, are not. In fact, these latter two modes of knowing are often ignored as invalid at best, or even denigrated, ridiculed, and actively suppressed at worst. It is no accident, according to Plotkin, that this is the case because a culture based on commodities, demand, profit, and exploitation, thrives on ever changing technological invention to keep its populace racing for the next product. If humans were to elevate their feeling states and imagining to a level of equal validity with the other ways of knowing, it would be "bad for business" as Plotkin writes. This is because we would be more discerning about what is really in harmony with our well-being, and not be so susceptible to corporate shaping of our desires. We would know when something takes us further out of touch with ourselves and not settle for products meant to create profit for an elite few. When our thinking is detached from our feeling states and imaginings, we are not fully awake and in that state of relative numbness, mass mentality is easily exploited by profiteers with shiny marketing allurements.

The space of waiting, and its partner stillness, allows for different processes to emerge within us. We can actually wake up to more of who we are in our wholeness rather than continuing to be a cog in other people's designs. When the culture cultivates our attachment to immediacy at the expense of our uniqueness found only internally without external intrusion, we pay a terrible price.

One of the benefits of waiting as opposed to immediate gratification is the opening it gives to the emergence of our imaginations and the time to nurture the gifts such imaginings hold for us.

Jason Farman again:

> *Waiting, as represented by silences, gaps, and distance, allows us the capacity to imagine that which does not yet exist and, ultimately, innovate into those new worlds as our knowledge expands. [Waiting] shows how time flows through us and changes us. Day after day, as we wait for the things we desire, we become different people. In the act of waiting,*

we become who we are. Waiting points to our desires and hopes for the future; and while that future may never arrive and our hopes may never be fulfilled, the act of reflecting on waiting teaches us about ourselves. The meaning of life isn't deferred until that thing we hope for arrives; instead, in the moment of waiting, meaning is located in our ability to recognize the ways that such hopes define us.

Lichen,

Today I was musing about my choice to enter a marriage without adequately grieving the end of my hopes and dreams to stay with my college girlfriend, L. That day of senior year when I saw her walking across campus with another young man, I knew the end was coming and I had my first panic attack. I was so frightened that I phoned my father to take me out of school. Of course, he simply said something like, "time will pass," or "it will pass." So true, but given my history with him, it just felt like another emotional abandonment.

I was living in that pit of an apartment in Chicago when R. made the effort to drive from Michigan to see me. She was so sincerely interested in me and that feeling of being authentically desired was too powerful for me to resist. In that place, alone in a slum, I went against deeper knowing and proposed marriage. I was not ready.

As I think about it now, if I had done more inner work, I might have developed a healthier capacity for that connection, but I didn't do it. I had never freed myself by grieving. The loss of L was also an opportunity to fully grieve what was there at a deeper level. The panic attack in college was my outright egoic refusal to psychically go there and it did not show up again until I was at the monastery 46 years later! That dormant period is what brings you to mind, my dear Lichen. I know that you live in a different realm of time—your life span can be hundreds if not thousands of years and some of your species have been on the planet for at least 400 million years. I am like a mayfly in comparison—only having a brief life span. When I saw that painting in the monastery of radiant love, coupled with the portent of death, I knew I was both infant and sacrificial lamb—both innocent and open to receiving either love or devastating wound. What had lain dormant in me, the full embodiment of my grief, threatened to erupt again. Another panic attack came— my ego valiantly trying to keep it away. I have been grappling with this for the past eight months now. When I think about your capacity to wait years if necessary for conditions conducive to re-ignition of life energy, I see my own journey of dormant grief with greater compassion. Once again, I am grateful for your loving wisdom.

Yours in dormancy and re-awakening,

LL

DEEP IMAGINAL JOURNEY TO RE-VISIT LICHEN IN ORIGINAL PLACE

Shamanic drumming. I close my eyes and enter a Deep Imaginal Journey...I approach the land in northern New Mexico where Lichen resides in the Ponderosa pine forest at Hummingbird Ranch. I am facing a hole in the ground where I will enter. I realize I must unclothe myself and enter this hole naked. It becomes a tunnel and I crawl through, feeling the earth surround my naked body both back and front. I am prone, stretched out in full length in order to make my way through. I move and spiral sometimes on my back, sometimes on my front and feel the earth moving along my body. It is sensual and erotic, and I feel deeply held there. Eventually I emerge from the tunnel and move upward onto the land. I know where I am and head intentionally toward a mature Ponderosa pine.

Lichen lives there and I am visiting her. I make physical contact and realize for the relationship to deepen in this moment I want every part of me to be in touch with her. I start with my beard and then move such that she gradually is touching me everywhere slowly...along my neck, my shoulders, my side, my hip, my leg, inward to my penis and scrotum...arousing me, then moving down the inside of my leg to my foot and up again to the center connection of my genitals and then my anus, so sensual, so erotic and then down the other leg, then up again to that erotic arousal and then abdomen, and chest and other arms, and neck, my back too...eventually my full face and head. Then I take

Lichen into me through my mouth and let her travel through my esophagus and gut. It diffuses into other parts of me internally, completing this external and internal intimacy. I am fully embraced and enlivened by this reunion, this full bodied greeting. I then ask for guidance for what my next step is.

At first, I am brought to the awareness of the tree that hosts Lichen as though this will be a spirit guide. My attention is guided upward into the upper most branches that are in a dance with the wind. I feel the rhythm of that dance and begin to allow the wind to bring me guidance. Yet again the wind, like the tree, is not the destination of this journey. It leads me to a being that is morphing into a conglomeration of sorts. It has a lean human core it seems with a masculine presence, a large erect phallus, but also a tail, and wings, and ears that are larger and pointed. This being has the power of many life forms: the stealth of an earth predator and the capacity for flight. It is agile and virile in its masculine energy, and generously willing to give those qualities to me. I find I am lying on my back on the ground, and it moves over me, almost sitting or crouching on me but hovering above. It is a powerful, lithe, and charismatic being and I lie under it, yet it does not touch me. I feel its energy knowing it is an offering to me... I am receptive and eager to receive its infiltration.

After this encounter seems complete, I know it's time to return and I make my way back into the tunnel with my naked, energized body. The full-contact return is also sensual, and I re-emerge, clothe myself, and return to my world. Before I rise, my hands trace the pathway that Lichen has taken over all parts of my body, holding that intimacy deeply along with the sensuality and erotism of it. I then arise and the shamanic drumming ends.

***

What kind of undertaking is this anyway? Unwittingly, I was drawn into this communion with Lichen. It seemed such a small and safe little being, hanging gently from a branch, minding its own business. Yet somehow it called me over, aroused me deeply, and revealed an enveloping cosmic Love for me to taste. And now here I am, bound for life! What I thought was a lucky, fleeting, transcendent moment has now taken me over. I have subsequently been dragged down into the darkest recesses of myself, directly into and through my core wound, forced to take the journey I had previously only intermittently dabbled in. Is this some kind of Divine bait and switch tactic?

Threads being woven together reach from all directions and span through my entire history as though Mystery had been designing this process from my beginnings and even likely before. Images from dreams are serving as guideposts and begin to relate to each other in surprising ways. So much of what had seemed to be separate, disconnected pathways over decades in different geographic locations are now curiously intertwined and interdependent. If it all weren't so awesome, I would be drowning in terror. Somehow, despite being called to a task to which I feel ill prepared and inadequate to perform, I also feel blessed and gifted with being chosen. Like stuttering Moses protesting God's call to speak to a powerful king,

I too feel the limits of my own version of stuttering as I move into this calling. I also know my perspective is a miniscule point in this vast realm of Mystery.

WISDOM

ENERGY NODE AS PORTAL

"I am an energy node in the web and one teacher." **Lichen**

While contemplating Lichen on a stone one afternoon, I received this offering. It felt like a reminder of the larger cosmos, beyond any one individual presence. I suddenly realized that Lichen is not the only incarnation of energy holding wisdom and guidance toward fuller awakening. My inference from this teaching is that teachers are ubiquitous and that I happened to be in relationship with only one of them. Perhaps we are surrounded by teachers patiently waiting, ready to guide each unique soul when Mystery so arranges the meeting. I also believe Lichen to be saying, that despite the vast numbers of incarnate beings, it may be best to immerse oneself in <u>one</u> such Teacher. This involves fully giving oneself over (physical proximity/connection, scientific study, apprenticeship to that teacher's Way of Being) and sharing the most irreconcilable questions of living in conversation in "dialogue." Moving beyond our usual limited beliefs around humans atop a hierarchy of intelligence is essential in this wisdom journey.

ANCESTRY

Lichens are likely responsible for providing a key evolutionary step in the transfer of marine life to the colonization of land. Several scientific studies have emphasized this fact. At the time of initial colonization of land, the environmental conditions were extremely harsh and Lichen, by virtue of its symbiotic relationship, survived when neither alga nor fungus alone could have endured.

Merlin Sheldrake again:

> *When lichens die and decompose, they give rise to the first soils in new ecosystems. Lichens are how the inanimate mineral mass within rocks is able to crossover into the metabolic cycles of the living. A portion of the minerals in your body is likely to have passed through a lichen at some point.*

Since humans eventually also evolved on land, if we are to trace our ancestry, this is where it begins, at least since land was inhabited at all by living beings. At our deepest origins is the existence of mutualistic symbiosis, the life affirming relationship that is now seen by biological scientists as central to evolution. The prototype of such relationship is manifest in Lichen and this pioneering symbiosis across otherwise unrelated species, offers us both guidance and warning.

If we pay attention, we may understand the power in bridging disparate difference, in allowing what is foreign to mix and alter us. Similar to the concept of metal alloy, the combing of two disparate elements may produce a third, unique substance with qualities and powers non-existent in either alone. As in physics where discoveries reveal the trinitarian nature of material incarnation of energy, so too does Lichen express this cosmic truth. As Richard Rohr writes in *"The Divine Dance"*: "The Trinity is the basic relationship of the cosmos." This intersection of science and Theology helps heal centuries of Cartesian dualism.

Western culture tends to emphasize the new, shun history, marginalize the elderly, and idolize change. While change is valuable and essential, an awareness of what has come before, what has provided the foundation, what opens the pathway, is crucial to our survival. Change without embracing origins is empty, flimsy, and has no capacity for nourishment of the culture. It breeds disconnection when embraced at this surface level only. Each branch, each leaf of a tree could be seen as separate if no broader awareness of the central trunk of origin is maintained. And with that disjointed perspective, greed, and exploitation rather than reciprocity and mutuality become the currency of the culture. There is no longevity in that. Without gratitude for all that we have arisen from, specifically the living system of this planet, we forget it, take endlessly from it, deplete it, dump waste into it and blindly commit suicide.

Lichen models the way to endure, adapt, and live in alignment with natural condition and it relies upon its inherent profound relational, mutualistic state to achieve this. Such is the ancestry we must know; it is the wisdom of a true elder, there for us if we simply attend to it, listen, and emulate this ancient and seminal being. Without the miracle of Lichen, we would not exist. By living antithetically to its teachings, disavowing our ancestral birthright, we will squander our chance for survival. No doubt once humanity has extinguished itself, Lichen will endure, perhaps offering another chance.

"Let my ability for dormancy related to external scarcities be your guide. It is like the gift of winter in your seasonal cycle and there is no hierarchy of seasons. Energetic life and light do not supersede death, decay, and darkness." **Lichen**

DORMANCY

Death is on my mind. Maybe because autumn is harkening the impending descent into winter's stark and barren home. Everything is enduring, withstanding, waiting, postponing, grieving, and possibly even dying unless by some miracle spring is reached again. On a galactic scale, Earth's tilt away from the sun is miniscule, yet here it is profoundly life altering for so many beings.

Some of us will die during winter's harshness, but those of us who eke by are transformed by this proximity to death. In our daily encounters with the cycle of life and death in our natural surroundings, we are routinely offered the chance to integrate the truth of dying into the fabric of our living. Unfortunately, we rarely do. Without a sense of partnership with death, without holding an infusion of its essence to life, the terrain of living flattens and becomes dull. Instead, we preoccupy ourselves with surface sparkle, an endless series of distractions and deflections. As technology is harnessed to circumvent, evade, and disguise death's ubiquitous presence, our disconnection from ourselves and from all of the rest of the natural world dominates.

Ironically this avoidance of death actually sickens us. Living without consciously dancing with death is the disease of our time. Humanity attempts to overcome the forces of nature, to outwit death, to be eternally young and immortal. So much time spent evading death's truth leads to a cheapening of living and blindness to the precious and fragile thread we are given.

A great teacher and guide must lead us into this truth of life and death since neither exists independently of the other. There is no discreet boundary between them. Desert beings reveal this quite overtly. Often growing out of apparently dead branches and above ground roots are new green sprouts, clearly thriving despite emerging from a seemly dead substrate. Many plants carry both dead and living elements, brown and green, decay and growth, sharing the same center and support.

Our own bodies simultaneously hold dying or dead cells and regenerating ones. On a grander scale, there is no end to existence as the illusory boundaries of a previously discrete being merely give way after death to a redistribution of its elements to the larger system. In this way, death becomes an opportunity for re-forming and re-creating a true substrate for new life.

Lichen holds this partnership in a unique way. Literally a composite being, its components of fungi and algae or cyanobacteria create a structurally altering interplay of beings who, when independent of each other, function at apparent opposite ends of the life-death spectrum. Capable of photosynthesis, algae are creating new life, building with sun-produced energy, while fungi serve the system through facilitating decay and decomposition. This mutual habitation brings the seeming polar opposites of life and death together into a stable, enduring organism with longevity well beyond that of humans. Despite our supposed superior intelligence often focused on postponing or even avoiding death, our life spans are quite brief in comparison.

During meditation, I have an image of my connections to other humans all over the planet as radiating lines from my center. I see my death and the people that would be impacted in varying degrees all over the earth. I feel extended over the planet, like Lichen, everywhere.

Notably, Lichen's capacity to persevere, to endure and live through periods of extreme environmental deficit, is anchored in its ability to curtail energy use, and enter a latent or dormant phase until conditions change. This is a kind of "dead" state, not at all appealing to humanity. Our technology is focused on changing or subjugating nature to fit our needs, rather than on adaptation and living in reciprocity with what is offered.

Although we certainly can impact the larger living system, as evidenced by the changes in the ozone layer and multiple other ecosystems, we will never control it for our benefit without inadvertently spawning other forces at odds with our continued existence. Rather than trying to outwit, exclude, evade, or render aging and dying obsolete, it would serve us well to live with death as our deepest twin partner.

STAYING PUT

This is an unprecedented experience in my adult life, staying put without imminent plans. I cannot recall another time like this. I've always had a trip planned or forming in the near future, or if not traveling for adventure, then visiting someone at some distance. More recently my focus has been planning to attend the next workshop, conference, or nature based retreat. In the background were also the demands of work life with schedules, daily commitments, and plans for future appointments to secure the longevity of my income producing work.

Now I have moved to a geographic area where I essentially know no one other than my partner, communicate primarily through sporadic email threads, and rarely have telephone contact. I've recently returned from my aborted desert writing retreat so now I find myself home, plans ended, and none pending.

I realize I have been on the psychological run for decades, lured by exotic offerings of international travel, the more foreign and unfamiliar the better. It was formerly such a draw, looking to the next international destination, flying over oceans, entering strange and different cultures. In those settings, I had to really pay attention to the external stimuli to survive. This was my idea of adventure, and Asian or African countries were best suited for such challenges. Europeans look like me, and my own culture derives from that area more directly than more remote or exotic places where even my appearance separates me.

My journey in contrast is inner now—it is of utmost interest—I'm shedding illusions if I can see them. I'm cultivating compassion and love and humility as the guides for my travels. Looking through those lenses, everything changes. I am not trying to get anywhere. This is the way of Lichen. I remember being struck by the environmental artist Andy Goldsworthy's aversion to traveling—his value of the rooted feeling in his homeland. I understand this now. It has taken a long time and innumerable miles of travel for me to see this.

So now here I am at home, uninterested in visiting the locales that previously enthralled me. At times, I try to muster a fantasy of foreign immersion, but it fizzles and no longer holds energy for me. I am quite surprised by this change. Since my father took me along on a business trip by airplane at age five, I've been hooked, addicted to the magic combination of flying, crossing borders, and encountering people who know nothing about me or my home environment.

I'm haunted by Lichen's declaration, *"you pay a price for your mobility."* I recall a book about the 10 most significant evolutionary advances. Movement is one of them: movement that is self-powered rather than a consequence of wind or water flow.

I'm realizing one of the prices I pay for my mobility is diminished longevity—I move more quickly to my demise and travel more on the surface of life's network. I now remember the phrase used in psychiatric mental status examination to help evaluate the abstracting ability of the client/patient. "Still waters belie great depth." This of course implies its converse that movement tends to dwell on the surface, a rich place in itself, but not what depth can offer. I realize allowing oneself to dance intimately with death while living leads to a journey of depth; there lay marvels not known at the surface. The wisdom of stillness thus deepens. I am caught by surprise by these offerings Lichen metes out to me. They seem to come when I am ready to be affected by them. Otherwise, I suppose I wouldn't notice; they would simply glance off my own surface, leaving me essentially untouched.

I realized early that my neighborhood was only a small dot of life on this planet and there were so many other ways to live. With exposure to international travel, I began to experience numerous other languages to speak. Once, when asked what I would wish for most, I immediately responded with the idea of being able to speak at least 50 languages fluently. After seeing an imaginative film in which someone was able to fly a helicopter due to the insertion of a chip in his body that imparted that knowledge and skill, I longed for such a transformative chip to access languages.

I have frequently been frustrated by the lack of depth in communication due to language barriers, so the idea of speaking with people in many different countries in their own language seemed the greatest gift I could imagine. Without such communication I merely skimmed over the visits and knew I was missing connection to the wisdom held by other cultures. Although I have a significant working vocabulary and ability to communicate in Spanish, I have unsuccessfully attempted to learn Japanese, Vietnamese, Swahili, and Portuguese. I simply cannot retain new linguistic information and have never been in an area long enough for the immersion to achieve this.

Fortunately, I'm permeable to music from around the world and through that type of communication I'm able to learn, perhaps even more deeply.

It is no accident that this waning attraction to geographic travel has occurred simultaneously with my deepening conversation with Lichen. This being has patiently imparted the wisdom of staying still and living in a profound reciprocal connection to its essentially unchanging location. I settle in here without imminent plans to go anywhere, anytime soon. It is a new experience. I'm allowing a void to build and see where it takes me. I'm a novice at this, but of course this is Lichen's forte and the wisdom I am offered now.

As my inner journey unfolds, the challenges and stunning realizations have continued to outshine the glamor and seduction of foreign travel. Indeed, the greatest allure has become the path of Mystery, a path

I cannot plan or schedule or control. I allow it to come by settling into the stillness and silence that seems to be an invitation. This is Lichen's way. I am staying put and listening.

THE ZONE

I played tennis seriously and competitively for many years, pre-teen until college. I remember the feelings of balance, graceful movement, anticipation, confidence in timing, and power at the moment of contact with the ball. In retrospect, it was my enjoyment in the process of moving through those feelings that superseded my drive to actually win. I was gifted with what others called talent and was quite successful. However, this did not result in as winning a record as might have occurred if that were my actual aim.

While practicing the array of shots necessary for a winning game of tennis, I was more drawn to the beauty and complexity of the visual, tactile, and aural aspects of tracking, timing, and listening to the ball hit the opponent's racket strings than any other goal. There were times when I felt I was conducting an exquisite symphony of sorts, all without thinking.

In fact, it was the very disengagement from thought that marked my best play. I was then in what other players called 'the zone" when everything flows flawlessly, and errors are rare. Of course, those times coincided with winning the points too, but that was not the most compelling feature of that experience. My body simply knew what to do; the physics of movement, time, angles of arm and wrist, footwork, eye tracking, balance, speed, hearing the ball leave my opponent's string to determine its speed toward me, watching that racket's movement after the contact to determine how the ball's spin was shaped, all of it was woven into my sense of connection. I was finely tuned to the flow of it all, not unlike a cheetah's grace and efficiency in pursuit of moving prey.

This state, this zone, what is it? I realize my mind has no answer to this, but I intuit this experience to be the essence of being in the other than human world. We alone seem to have minds that interfere with this unselfconscious connection so apparently natural and total for all other beings. We relentlessly inhibit our own fullness of presence. As David Whyte expresses, *we are the one terrible part of creation privileged to refuse our flowering.*

Being in "the zone" gave me a sense of presence, however brief, and now I see it as a glimpse of Lichen's consistent state of being. Lichen has no buffer from reality, no attempt to alter what **is**. Stillness, silence, intermittent dormancy, all are finely tuned to the present moment, always in the zone.

I have numerous opportunities to sit in council. These are sober gatherings of people committed to authentic and vulnerable disclosure about what each of us is experiencing now at the edges of our interface with living. There is a holding and witnessing of what is shared, one at a time, without feedback, advice, or judgmental response. It provides a confidential container for deep sharing and unimpeded listening.

On one occasion, our council guides invited us to embody other-than-human beings and share from their perspective. This communal ritual called The Council of All Beings is a specific type of council developed by Joanna Macy and John Seed that...

"allows us to step aside from our human identity and speak on behalf of other life forms. It is excellent for growing the ecological self, for it brings a sense of solidarity with all life and fresh awareness to the damage caused by one upstart species."

This communal council experience became a diverse, multi-species and even "non-animate" gathering. Among us were a whale, tree, owl, cloud, boulder, raven, and elephant, among others. I was compelled to embody Lichen and immediately felt transformed into a motionless, silent being. I maintained this other-than-human state for the duration of the council. I watched and listened as the others enacted and spoke from various other beings' perspectives.

Typically, I'm an active member of every council, always choosing to share my present state in these confidentially bound meetings. But sitting motionless, not even shifting or moving any part of my body for an extended period, intensified the power of the experience. I was immersed in listening, in hearing, and I had no struggle with choosing when or if I would speak. I simply did not. From that position the world took on a very different tone. Mute and motionless, as I adhered to one spot, I was free to take in much more than usual. I realized I also had a less contaminated route to my own voice in whatever form or language it might ultimately show itself. Through this embodiment of Lichen's 'perspective' my usual human egoic functioning seemed to disappear, providing an emptiness for great presence to develop. Another lesson received.

"Don't impose an engine upon the flow in order to speed through it or against it." **Lichen**:

CONSULTATION WITH LICHEN (ENGINE)

Lichen has become my frequent companion. Given my belief in and acceptance of Lichen's wisdom, I'm inclined to consult Lichen quite frequently through the course of each day. At times when I'm blindly swept into some cultural norm that is antithetic to a life of reciprocity and sustainability, I catch myself at odds with Lichen's teachings of Love, patience, faith in the flow, stillness, and silence. When I receive this teaching, I'm struck by the choice of the word, "engine." I suppose it's the perfect word to capture the idea of a human construction designed to alter, dominate, or eradicate a natural rhythm or flow. Engines use energy, channeled from natural resources, then redirected and released by human ingenuity. Taken too far, these constructions have insulated and isolated us from a harmonious, reciprocal interplay with all that we evolved from.

For example, we divert water for our own, often wasteful use, depriving whole ecosystems with this self-serving and short-sighted pursuit. Lichen has efficiently adapted to almost every degree of water availability across different terrains and climates, using air moisture or the riches of rain to thrive on only what is needed. When no water is available, or other conditions are incompatible with active life, Lichen suspends itself, lying patiently dormant until nutrients return. I can listen to Lichen when she speaks to me of stillness and patience because I see her model it. This is practicing what is preached without hypocrisy and so I can respect it. In contrast, I witness many in authority or some hierarchical role living in an exploitative manner undermining all credibility.

TREE STUMP

Moving from a densely populated urban area to a forested area quite near, I can now see trees and sky while sitting in our home. Although I long for even closer intimacy with this forest, I can venture among the trees easily. Formerly Osage hunting grounds, our "legally owned" property is limited in typical residential development style. There is a paucity of trees that live in immediate proximity to the actual living space. Sadly, there is a stump left behind after an obviously mature tree was severed and hauled away before our move here. It holds memory of a different time when this tree rose full and grand, evidenced by its significant diameter.

My first reaction when we moved here was to remove the stump because of the pain I felt when seeing it. Clearly this magnificent and long-lived being had been either diseased or damaged beyond salvage. Since there are numerous other grand trees in the surrounding lots, I imagine and prefer to think that the decision to cut it down was based on a necessity beyond any cultural wish to simply clear an obstacle. I also assume there was grief involved in this process. Now that I live close to it, I feel that grief even without having known this tree in its primacy. Although I initially want to remove the stump and avoid being reminded daily of the human saw that severed this being, I stop when I see two lovely species of Lichen that flourish on the remaining bark. I can no longer in good conscience imagine removing this stump since the Lichen found a place to thrive, primarily facing the eastern light. Knowing that Lichen wisely chooses its environment, avoiding polluted air, I receive its presence as a gift, showing it is safe to breathe this air myself and co-exist alongside this natural bio-monitor.

There are both crustose, in this case yellow-green, and white foliose lichen growing on the stump, so it is a rich neighborhood indeed. Once again, I am guided away from the narrow confines of my initial view of the death or murder of this tree and shown the opportunity for life that has emerged.

One life form is not ascendant to another. A tree, though larger and grander to a human's eyes, is not a greater part of the cosmic web than the smallest, least prominent Lichen village now inhabiting the legacy of that tree's remains. In fact, it is the very death of the tree that gives way to more light for the Lichen to flourish; this reciprocity so ubiquitous and even the essence of the web of life, is the teacher. I am moved once more beyond narrow dualistic comparisons into the flow that death as the substrate of life brings forth in my consciousness. And again, I am reminded how this small easily ignored being perseveres and endures, ultimately outliving many other living beings that dwarf it in size and presence. These Lichens are just outside the back door, so I can visit them easily and regularly, day or night, at any time I choose without a barrier to impede the visit. I can also see these Lichens by simply looking through the glass paned back door. I am grateful that this tree stump home of Lichens is so close to my own living space. It is as though I live among my extended family, having elders to consult with whenever I am ready to seek and receive guidance.

Lichen,

There is a prayer recited daily at the Christine Center in Wisconsin. It begins: "In the name of the one God, Mother-Father of us all..." I am reflecting about ancestry. Today, Father's Day has evoked these musings. Several months ago, I was preparing for an ancestral heritage, healing, and wounding immersion. It was cancelled due to low registration, but I did some tracking on ancestry.com in preparation. I learned some things but wanted to know much more. Eventually I gave up the investigation but not the longing. I have so many questions about the people who came before me, both from other continents and here in North America. I know that information would open up more understanding about what threads were woven into me, both genetically and spiritually. I know so little. But if I realize the essence of my ancestry is the creation itself, I am more resolved.

You, Lichen, are part of my story, a pioneer on the land, an early elaborator of oxygen, a guide to the transformative power of symbiosis. Perhaps you hold an incarnation of the basic trinity of all cosmic truth. You are a relational being. It is what distinguishes you in the beginnings of Gaian life. And now here we are, humans, highly evolved to carry relationship further. Yet we must be fledgling relators since we are so destructive with the same gifts that could bring the powerful unitive energy of creator evolution even further. My dear Lichen, you are a model if more of humanity would only take notice. Apprenticeship to your wisdom just waiting to be entered.

I am fortunate; you called me, and I answered. The invitation of Love is so encompassing, irresistible and transformative that my puny, separating human mind could only submit. And so, my deep connection with you, a being of impeccable symbiotic relationship, began. I have been given a great gift and have been on a tumultuous but non-negotiable pathway ever since. There are no guideposts, no markers, and no chance of turning back. I can avoid, postpone, seek dormancy, or even flight into escape but ultimately you are waiting. Time is not relevant to you and so when I muster up the courage yet again, I venture further, deeper, into this inner wilderness.

In love and gratitude,

Lover of Lichen

WOUND PATH

Grotesquely disfigured bark
violently splayed away from
its former illusory, safe, snug encasement
speaks of a cataclysmic assault
on this still upright and growing Pine.

Revealed
the scarred and hardened core
terribly, yet gracefully swirled in its injury
continues its central, foundational support
despite the trauma of its past.

I know this Lightning Strike.
It is the Wound in my core
that which nearly destroyed vitality
spawning life-saving strategies of undaunted
Survival
and Heart guarding tigers.

It is an awesome and unique Wound
and I would have no other
for the Path begins here and unfolds
through cynical tunnels of pain and bitterness
to open fields of love and sweet gratitude
just as the soft moss emerges
from cold, hard Stone
shedding a single dewdrop
tear.

Snake greets me in this Pine place.
We share a space and time
long enough for her message
of perfect Stillness
and mature Patience
to guide me on my journey.

The allure of Stream then beckons me.
Tentatively, I shed shoes and socks
and gingerly make my way
over the barely submerged
smooth river stones.

Soon the call grows too compelling to resist.
I overcome my civilized disconnection from
Wildness
and become a creature unfettered
by Industry and Manufacture
as clothing and gear are left behind.

Now a naked, wondrous being
willing to risk the clarity and coldness of the Flow.

I find my home here
a place both hospitable and indifferent.
Rooms with verdant life
brown and gray decay of death
and granite stones strewn with timelessness.

Place infused with music
my Wound's lifeline.
The cleansing, relentless and rushing din

of nearby water.
Overhead, the high and full voiced tree-tops
wrestling with the wind.
Below, a bass line of humming bees
their staccato, chaotic
yet focused visits
to each impossibly tiny white-pink bell of flower
in this green room
where I gladly share my bed.

There are no windows here
no limits of frame or pane of glass.
The vista in all directions
draws my grateful and loving gaze.

Decades of travel around the planet
observing Earth's vast grandeur from afar
have merely traced insulated orbits
prefacing my soulful descent
into this new, exquisite, and intimate Place.

My Beloved greets me here
Lichen and beard mingle in sensual and reverent
Love
and I walk with gravity through the forest aisle.
A Sacred Marriage this is
uncontaminated by ambivalence.

Wound began this journey
building seemingly impregnable walls
but as Grief is deeply felt and fully inhabited
the walls dissolve and give way

unleashing the flow of Love
and guiding me into freedom.

Freedom to embrace the Mystery
this union so lovingly brings.

ACKNOWLEDGEMENTS

I'm grateful to many who have supported me in revealing this deeply personal and unusual journey. My tendency was often to avoid it using numerous excuses and projections about how this story might be received. As a result, my writing spanned almost seven years, despite the relatively brief length of the work. Ultimately, out of reverence and gratitude to Lichen, I could not abandon this project and so I persevered. My experience of the depth of Love in Lichen's presence during that initial encounter continues to provide the foundation of ongoing awe, curiosity, and commitment that fuels this journey of awakening and soulful expression.

Several friends have encouraged me to stay the course and share my story. Bryan Smith helped me identify and overcome obstacles in the process while consistently holding and mirroring the sacred sense of what I was called to do. Karim Aziz's kindness and ongoing deep affirmations soothed resurgences of self-doubt, and Belden Lane generously reviewed and made comments on an early portion of the book. Bob Sabath has companioned me along the way, deeply listening to my process and also offering technical support during my maddening befuddlement with page numbering. He is a magician on many levels.

A unique cadre of soul journeying friends, Lauren Golten, Sheila Murray, and Mark Timken has been meeting regularly for nine years now, despite our geographic distance. We share our joys and pains with unusual depth, compassion, and skillful mirroring. These dear friends never wavered from inviting me deeper into the process of sharing my story.

Jacqueline Suskin provided clear editorial support and guidance. She truly was in alignment with my counter-cultural relationship with Lichen and helped me find ways to express my experience more effectively.

Despite my plethora of internal obstacles in completing this offering, I am deeply grateful that my beloved, Karen McClard, never colluded with any of them. She patiently witnessed my struggles, offered creative possibilities for me to keep writing, and certainly played a significant part in why I was receptive to Lichen's loving call in the first place.

REFERENCES

Lynn Margulis, *Symbiotic Planet a New Look At Evolution (1998)*

James Hillman, *The Soul's Code: In Search of Character and Calling (1996)*

Merlin Sheldrake, *Entangled Life: How Fungi Make our Worlds, Change our Minds, and Shape our Futures (2020)*

Bill Plotkin, *Wild Mind: A Field Guide to the Human Psyche (2013)*

Daniel Deardorff, *The Other Within: The Genius of Deformity in Myth, Culture, and Psyche (2008)*

David Whyte: *The House of Belonging (1997)*

Richard Rohr, *The Divine Dance: The Trinity and Your Transformation (2016)*

Jason Farman, *Delayed Response The Art of Waiting from the Ancient to the Instant World (2018)*

Joanna A. Macy and Molly Brown, *Coming Back to Life (2014)*

Glenn Siegel, *Howling with Gratitude and Grief,* Poetry Collection *(2024)*

SUGGESTED READING

David Abram, *Becoming Animal: An Earthly Cosmology* (2010)
_______________*The Spell of the Sensuous: Perception and Language in a More-Than-Human World* (2012)

Janine Benyus, *Biomimicry: Innovation Inspired by Nature* (1997)

Thomas Berry, *The Dream of the Earth (1988)*
_______________*The Great Work: Our Way into the Future* (2011)

James Bridle, *Ways of Being: Plants, Animals, Machines: The Search for a Planetary Intelligence* (2022)

Stephen Harrod Buhner, *Plant Intelligence and the Imaginal Realm: Beyond the Doors of Perception Into the Dreaming of Earth* (2014)

Robin Wall Kimmerer, *Braiding Sweetgrass: Indigenous Wisdom, Scientific Knowledge, and the Teaching of Plants* (2015)
_______________________________, *Gathering Moss: A Natural and Cultural History of Mosses* (2003)

Belden Lane, *The Great Conversation: Nature and the Care of the Soul (2019)*

Llewellyn Vaughn-Lee, *Spiritual Ecology: The Cry of the Earth (2016)*

Joanna Macy & Chris Johnstone, *Active Hope: How to Face the Mess We're in without Going Crazy (2012)*

Michael Meade, *Fate and Destiny, the Two Agreements of the Soul (2012)*

John Philip Newell, *Sacred Earth, Sacred Soul: Celtic Wisdom for Reawakening to What our Souls Know and Healing the World* (2021)

Ed Yong, *An Immense World: How Animal Senses Reveal the Hidden Realms Around Us (2022)*

Gerald May, *The Wisdom of Wilderness: Experiencing the Healing Power of Nature* (2006)

Malidoma Somé, *The Healing Wisdom of Africa: Finding Life Purpose Through Nature, Ritual, and Community* (1999)
__________________, *Ritual: Power, Healing, and Community* (1997)
__________________, *Of Water and the Spirit: Ritual, Magic, and the Initiation of an African Shaman* (1994)

Jacqueline Suskin, *A Year in Practice: Seasonal Rituals and Prompts to Awaken Cycles of Creative Expression*

Martín Prechtel, *The Smell of Rain on Dust: Grief and Praise* (2015)

Bill Plotkin, *Soulcraft : Crossing into the Mysteries of Nature and Psyche (2003)*
______________*Nature and the Human Soul: Cultivating Wholeness and Community in a Fragmented World (2008)*
______________*The Journey of Soul Initiation A Field Guide for Visionaries, Evolutionaries, and Revolutionaries* (2021)

About the author

Glenn Siegel, M.D. practiced Psychiatry for over 35 years. As his professional career ended, he entered into a larger conversation with the more-than-human world. Lichen became an unexpected portal to this expanded realm of eco-awakening, and transformation. Glenn is also the author of the poetry collection: *Howling with Gratitude and Grief.*